HOW THEN

CAN WE BE FRIENDS?

Written by Kayla Ferris
with contributions from the First 5 Team

We must exchange whispers with God before shouts with the world.

LYSA TERKEURST

Pair your Study Guide with the First 5 mobile app!

This Study Guide is designed to accompany your study of Scripture in the First 5 mobile app. You can use it as a standalone study, or as an accompanying guide to the daily content within First 5.

First 5 is a free mobile app developed by Proverbs 31 Ministries to transform your daily time with God.

Go to the app store on your smartphone, download the First 5 app and create a free account!

WWW.FIRST5.ORG

Welcome to Philippians

In the beginning, God created a single human. Yet God Himself — being Father, Son and Spirit — is community. He was not satisfied with creation until He also shared with man the joy of relationships. And since we are created in God's image, we have within us a built-in desire for community. Our longing for relationship and friendship is by design.

Which is great ... until it's not. Because let's be honest, sometimes relationships are just plain hard. We are all flawed people, and even when we are at our best, we are filled with different ideas, thoughts and opinions. Sometimes painful words are said. Sometimes differences seem too large to overcome. And we start to ask the question: *"How, then, can we be friends?"*

Maybe you've written off friendship. You've been hurt in the past, and it feels too risky. Maybe you really want friendship, but you can't seem to find it. There have been points in my life where I have felt all of these. Relationships are not always easy. But they are worth fighting for.

The book of Philippians is unlike any other book of the Bible. Within this letter, we get a rare glimpse into the close friendship of Paul and the church of Philippi. No other book has the language and warmth of relationship like Philippians. And by studying the relationships within this book, we are going to learn so much about friendship.

Chapter 1 will teach us that friendship is a source of joy, and that working together is the best way to advance the gospel.

Chapter 2 will teach us that the key to any relationship is to be humble, just like Jesus. We'll also see two examples of loyal and faithful friends.

Chapter 3 will remind us of what really matters: Jesus Christ. When we have friends with this common goal in mind, all other differences begin to fade in comparison.

Chapter 4 will show us that, yes, disagreements happen, but we can try to work through them. Chapter 4 also highlights generosity as a hallmark of true friendship.

We were created to be in community. Even when relationships are difficult — and they often will be — friendship is possible. And it's worth it.

Let's allow God's Word to speak life into our relationships. With His Word in hand, we can joyfully trust our friendships to Christ.

Who Wrote Philippians?

The book of Philippians is a personal letter between the Apostle Paul and a church that was very dear to him. In some ways, it is like a thank-you note. Paul's friends in Philippi supported him, and he wanted to show his appreciation. But Philippians is more than a thank-you. When we approach Philippians by reading it as a letter between friends, the words and context truly come alive.

This friendship between Paul and the church at Philippi began on Paul's second missionary journey. As Paul and his ministry partner Timothy were deciding where to travel, Scripture says the Holy Spirit forbade them to speak the word in Asia, then forbade them from going into Bithynia. (Acts 16:6-7) As they wandered around, trying to figure out what to do, Paul had a God-ordained vision. He saw a Macedonian man saying, *"Come over to Macedonia and help us"* (Acts 16:9). One of the leading cities of Macedonia? Philippi. You might say this friendship was providential.

However, the time spent in Philippi was not easy. Paul was captured, beaten with rods and thrown into prison. This did not deter Paul from praising God, and it eventually led to the conversion of a Philippian jailer. Ultimately, Paul was released and went on his way. He would return to Philippi for a quick stop on his third missionary journey.

Because Paul mentions being imprisoned in his letter, most scholars believe that this particular letter was written after Paul's third missionary journey. And because of his references to the *"imperial guard"* (Philippians 1:13) and *"Caesar's household,"* (Philippians 4:22) many think it was written while he was in Rome. This would date the letter to around A.D. 60-62.

Let's then sum up what we know. The time Paul spent in Philippi was rough. He was in a Roman prison, awaiting his trial, which could possibly lead to his death. How might you expect this letter to feel? Would you expect overflowing joy? Unfathomable peace? Warmth and love and gratitude? Probably not. Yet this is exactly what we find in this letter between friends.

In Christ, relationships are born. We meet people along our life journeys. The circumstances are not always easy. We might not even agree on every detail. (Philippians 3:15) But through Jesus, we are better together. We can have joy when others succeed. We can be grateful when others help us along the way. We can encourage and lift each other up because the tie that binds us together is Christ.

The History and Culture of Philippi

Today, ruins of the ancient city of Philippi can be found in modern-day Greece. Philippi was once an important city in the province of Macedonia. It was named after Philip of Macedon, the father of Alexander the Great. During Roman occupation, Philippi was the site of a decisive battle between the armies loyal to the murdered Julius Caesar and the armies led by Brutus and Cassius. As leader of the loyal armies, Octavian was the victor. Octavian became Augustus Caesar, and to commemorate his victory, he designated the city of Philippi as a Roman colony.

Being a Roman colony was quite the honor at that time. There were numerous benefits, such as the potential for land ownership and significantly lower taxes. It was also occupied by army veterans after they retired from service. Perhaps the greatest honor in being declared a Roman colony was that it gave the colonists Roman citizenship. Roman citizenship came with its own set of benefits, but even more, it came with respect and pride. [1] This may have been why Paul wanted to remind the Philippians that their most important citizenship was in heaven. (Philippians 3:20)

The church in Philippi was the first church Paul founded in Europe, and the very first convert of this church was a businesswoman named Lydia. (Acts 16:11-15) Christians in Philippi faced many struggles. Archaeologists have discovered the ruins of ancient temples to pagan gods, specifically to Apollo and Artemis. It is apparent that pagan worship was fluid during the earliest days of the church because when Paul and Silas cast out a demon from a slave girl who told fortunes, her owners became upset and had them thrown into prison. (Acts 16:16-24) We can also conclude that there was a Jewish population within the city. Not all Jews were open to Christianity, and of those who were, many tried to enforce Jewish customs, such as circumcision, on new gentile believers. (Philippians 3:2) There were many dangers to the growing church in Philippi.

However, this did not seem to stop them. The church in Philippi would be marked for its generosity. Paul said *"no church entered into partnership with me in giving and receiving, except you only"* (Philippians 4:15). Paul spoke of the churches in Macedonia when he said, *"for in a severe test of affliction, their abundance of joy and their extreme poverty have overflowed in a wealth of generosity on their part"* (2 Corinthians 8:2). They might have been tested, afflicted and poor, but they had joy!

Generosity and joy in the face of trials. Paul demonstrated it when he joyfully wrote this letter from prison. The Philippians revealed it in their joyful support of the gospel in a hostile culture.

Themes in Philippians

FRIENDSHIP

Philippians is unique from any of Paul's other letters because it is warm and personable. These were truly dear friends he was writing. As a friend, he prays for them, encourages them, and talks about how he misses them. He held them in his heart (Philippians 1:7) and called them his *"joy and crown"* and his *"beloved"* (Philippians 4:1). As Christ-followers, we too are called to friendship with other believers. We, too, can stand firm *"in one spirit, with one mind striving side by side for the faith of the gospel"* (Philippians 1:27).

JOY

The word *"joy"* or *"rejoice"* appears 14 times in this short letter. Christians have so many reasons for joy. Knowing Jesus and His love gives us a reason to rejoice! Godly friends and community are a source of joy. We can even rejoice in our trials, because we can trust God to complete the good work He started in us. In Philippians 2:17-18, Paul says, *"... I am glad and rejoice with you all. Likewise you also should be glad and rejoice with me."* I rejoice with you. You rejoice with me. Together we rejoice in Jesus! And just in case we missed it, Philippians 4:4 says, *"again I will say it, rejoice."*

LIVING LIKE JESUS

Philippians 1:27 says *"Let your manner of life be worthy of the gospel of Christ ..."* How do we live a life worthy of the gospel? Only by living like Jesus. And when we look at Jesus, we will see a humble servant. A servant who thought of others before His own interests. A servant who took on the shame of the cross. But we also see a servant who was lifted high, higher, in fact, than any other! (Philippians 4:9) In Christ, we get to share in His victory. We can *"press on toward the goal"* and know our *"citizenship is in heaven and from it we await a Savior, the Lord Jesus Christ, who will transform our lowly body to be like his glorious body ..."* (Philippians 3:14, 20-21).

TRANSFORMATION

At one point in Philippians, Paul lists his human credentials, and they are impressive. Yet Paul says *"I ... count them as rubbish"* because the only thing Paul considered of *"surpassing worth"* was *"knowing Christ Jesus [the] Lord"* (Philippians 3:8). Paul knew what it was like to be hungry and have plenty, yet he said he had learned that whatever situation he was in, he could *"be content"* (Philippians 4:11). The secret to this kind of contentment? Jesus. Jesus is all we could want and everything we could need. No matter what this life brings, in both life and death, we have everything if we have Christ. In Jesus, we, too, can say, *"... to live is Christ, and to die is gain"* (Philippians 1:21).

A Biblical Look at Joy

Because joy is a large part of the book of Philippians, let's take a larger look at joy in our Bible. We can learn so much about what true, biblical joy looks like when we search the Word and write what we gather.

BIBLE VERSE (with joy emphasized)	We learn that JOY IS:
*"For you make him most blessed forever; you make him glad with the **joy** of your presence."* - Psalm 21:6	Found in God's presence
*"A **joyful** heart is good medicine, but a crushed spirit dries up the bones."* - Proverbs 17:22	Good medicine
*"Shout, and sing for **joy**, O inhabitant of Zion, for great in your midst is the Holy One of Israel."* - Isaiah 12:6	A catalyst for praise
*"Your words were found, and I ate them, and your words became to me a **joy** and the delight of my heart, for I am called by your name, O Lord, God of hosts."* - Jeremiah 15:16	Found by ingesting God's Word and knowing who we are
*"… the **joy** of the Lord is your strength."* - Nehemiah 8:10	Strength
*"Just so, I tell you, there is **joy** before the angels of God over one sinner who repents."* - Luke 15:10	Found in repentance
*"These things I have spoken to you, that my **joy** may be in you, and that your **joy** may be full."* - John 15:11 (words from Jesus)	A gift from Jesus' own heart
*"But the fruit of the Spirit is love, **joy**, peace, …"* - Galatians 5:22	A fruit of the Holy Spirit in us
*"Count it all **joy**, my brothers, when you meet trials of various kinds, …"* - James 1:2	Found amid trials
*"Though you have not seen him, you love him. Though you do not now see him, you believe in him and rejoice with **joy** that is inexpressible and filled with glory, …"* - 1 Peter 1:8	Rooted in faith
*"So also you have sorrow now, but I will see you again, and your hearts will rejoice, and no one will take your **joy** from you."* - John 16:22 (words from Jesus)	One day ours forever!

Reading List and Major Moments

WEEK 1

"Indeed, I count everything as loss because of the surpassing worth of knowing Christ Jesus my Lord."

Philippians 3:8

Philippians 1:1-2

PAUL OPENED HIS LETTER BY GREETING THE CHURCH IN PHILIPPI.

In elementary school, I learned one way to begin a letter: return address, date, salutation. Our study in Philippians begins with a letterhead also. While the opening of this particular letter is standard style for Paul, each word used has significance when we look closely.

To begin, a letter would start with the name of the sender.

- Who are the two senders of this letter?

Paul wrote an astonishing 13 books (or letters) in the New Testament. He was used by God to spread the good news of Jesus to gentiles and surrounding nations. Paul took three major missionary journeys in his lifetime. He met the believers in Philippi on his second missionary journey. While we do not know the exact date this letter was written, most scholars believe it was written from Rome after Paul's third journey was complete.

- What do we know about Paul's situation in Rome when he wrote this letter? (See Philippians 1:13)

Timothy had met and joined Paul's work early into his second missionary journey. Therefore, he would have known the believers in Philippi as well. Let's take a moment to get to know Timothy.

- What do you learn about Timothy from Acts 16:1-3?

- What do you learn about his character from Philippians 2:19-22?

Let's take a look at two particular words used in the opening.

- In Philippians 1:1, Paul and Timothy are referred to as "_____ *of Christ Jesus.*"

- The intended audience of the letter is *"all the* _____ *in Christ Jesus ...*"

According to theologian David Chapman's commentary on Philippians, the Greek word for "servants," douloi, referred to "slaves." The Greek word for "saints," hagios, is the plural of the Greek word "holy." [2] Sometimes we think of leaders in the church as being extra holy, and the rest of us are lowly servants. God's Word reminds us that ALL Christ-followers, even leaders, are servants to Christ, and all are made holy because of Christ.

- The opening to Philippians demonstrates the humility that will be addressed later. Read Philippians 2:3. How does the use of *"servant"* and *"saint"* in 1:1 reflect what is taught in 2:3?

Finally, the letter opening finishes with the standard Christian salutation of the time. You can see a similar line in most of Paul's letters, as well as letters by Peter and John.

- Fill in the blanks to the salutation: "_____ to you and _____ from God our Father and the Lord Jesus Christ" (Philippians 1:2).

Historically, during this time period, Greek letters often began with a salutation that used the Greek word chairein or *"greetings."* Christians, like Paul, modified this opening to the word charis or *"grace."* [3]

- How is the word "grace" an appropriate Christian greeting? (Hint: What unites us as Christ-followers?)

Paul and Timothy worked side by side and had developed a close relationship to the church in Philippi.

- Take a moment to think about the friends and acquaintances in your life. How would you describe those relationships?

One final question (yet probably the most important!)

- Whose name appears three times in the two verses of today's reading?

Philippians 1:3-6

FRIENDS IN THE LORD ARE A JOY.

To fully appreciate what is being said in today's reading, let's put the situation into context.

- As a reminder, what was Paul's situation when he was writing this letter? (Philippians 1:13)

- In Acts 16, we learn a little about Paul's time spent in Philippi on his second missionary journey. Read Acts 16:22-24. How had Paul been treated in Philippi?

You might be familiar with the saying "out of sight, out of mind." According to God's Word, this saying does not apply to our relationships with others in Christ. According to Philippians 1:3, Paul remembered the people of Philippi.

- What specifically did Paul do when he remembered? (v. 3)

- Who is someone you haven't seen in a while that you could stop and thank God for right now?

- Paul says he remembers them, is thankful for them and prays for them with what? (v. 4)

Joy is a major theme throughout Philippians. This is just the first of 14 uses of the word in this short book. Joy is much more than happiness. As Paul's life shows, joy can be found despite circumstances.

- According to Psalm 16:11, where is joy found?

We also are given a glimpse into the source of this joy in Philippians 1:5. Paul prays with joy ...

- Fill in the blank: *"because of your _____ in the gospel ..."*

The Greek word is *koinōnia*. It means a close type of relationship, with a common interest or goal. It can also refer to a special type of fellowship known as "friendship." Even Greek philosopher Aristotle once said, "All friendship involves koinōnia." [4]

- According to Philippians 1:5, this *koinōnia* (or partnership) is rooted in the what?

- How might the good news of Jesus Christ (the gospel) strengthen the bonds of friendship and fellowship?

Paul remembered his friends with thankfulness. When he did, he said a prayer with joy. God's Word goes on to remind us of something immensely important about our friends and ourselves.

- Read Philippians 1:6. Who began a work in us?

- What kind of work is it?

- When will it be complete?

- What does that completion date remind us about our work right now?

We are all works in progress. We all need the grace of Jesus. Remembering this might help us show a little more grace to others as well.

- What does Ephesians 4:32 remind us?

Philippians 1:7-11

THROUGH CHRIST, WE CAN LOVE OUR FRIENDS WELL.

Yesterday, we learned that friends and fellowship in Christ are a source of great joy. Today, we will learn, through the example of Paul and the Philippians, how we can love our friends well.

- In Philippians 1:7, Paul says it is right for him to feel *"this way,"* referring to his joy and thankfulness, (vv. 3-4) for the Philippians because he holds them where?

The Greek word for "heart," *kardia*, was about more than emotion. It also involved the mind. It was intellectual. [5] Paul not only had good feelings toward his friends. He also had good thoughts. Bible scholar Matthew Henry once said, "It is very proper to think the best of other people, and as well as we can of them — to suppose as well of them as the matter will admit in all cases." [6]

- Do you tend to assume the best, or the worst, in the people around you? Why might that be the case?

Paul holds his friends dear in both thought and feeling for several reasons. Let's look at each.

- *"... I hold you in my heart, for you are all _____ with me of grace ..."* (Philippians 1:7)

- Write a definition for the word "partakers." Now try to sum up that definition in one word that could also describe friendship.

"... you are all partakers with me in grace, both in my _____ ..."

- According to the *ESV Study Bible*, "Paul's imprisonment would have been a source of great shame in the ancient world, but the Philippians have nonetheless stood in solidarity with him." [7] What does this say about friendship?

"... you are all partakers with me in grace, both in my imprisonment and in the defense and confirmation of the _____."

- What is one of the greatest things we can share among friends?

- *"For God is my witness, how I yearn for you all with the _____ of _____ _____" (Philippians 1:8).*

- Theologian Eugene Peterson says it like this: "Sometimes I think I feel as strongly about you as Christ does!" [8] Jot down what you think that might look like, to love your friends as much as Christ does.

After expressing his own love, Paul moves to a prayer for his friends, where he prays that their *"love might abound more and more"* (Philippians 1:9).

- Let's examine what love is from a biblical perspective. Beside each verse, write what you learn about love.

- 1 John 4:19

- John 15:13

- Romans 12:10

- 1 Corinthians 13:4-7

Love is an important part of the Christian faith. Here in Philippians 1:9, we are given two key words to help us understand how to love.

- *"And it is my prayer that your love may abound more and more with _____ and all _____."*

As Eugene Peterson put it, "...not only love much but well." [9]

Real love takes **knowledge**. We have to know the people we are loving in order to love them well.

Real love takes **discernment**. The Greek term for "discernment," *aisthēsis*, refers to the ability to make decisions for the benefit of others. [10] We have to discern others' needs. Ultimately, we have to discern God's calling on when and how to love.

- How might knowledge and discernment in love make our friendships better?

When we love better, we become better people. Philippians 1:10 says it helps us to *"be pure and blameless for the day of Christ."* This does not mean we suddenly become perfect. Rather, we are becoming a little more like Jesus. And becoming more like Jesus is a process that, over time, will cultivate the *"fruit of righteousness"* (Philippians 1:11). When we love others well, we will have better relationships, and we will become more like our Savior.

- But bearing this fruit is not of our own doing. It only comes through Who? (verse 11)

- And Who gets the glory for it?

Philippians 1:12-14

PAUL'S IMPRISONMENT HELPED ADVANCE THE GOSPEL.

The sentence *"I want you to know …"* (Philippians 1:12) serves as a transition. This section is directed toward the "brothers" in the church, but the Greek term used here, *adelphoi*, refers to both male and female believers. [11] Paul wants the Philippian believers to understand something important about *"what has happened to [him] …"*

According to verses 13 and 14, what had happened to Paul?

Paul was arrested in Jerusalem in A.D. 57 after his third missionary journey. In A.D. 60, he was transferred to Rome. For at least two years, Paul remained a prisoner there. Roman imprisonment was a holding place until the accused could have their trial or be executed. During this time, Paul was still able to live in his own private lodging, receive guests and write letters. (Acts 28:30-31) Because Paul was awaiting trial with the emperor, Paul had been delivered to the captain of the Praetorian Guard. The Praetorian Guard was the best of the Roman army and served as Caesar's own personal army. During Roman imprisonment, a guard would have been chained from his own wrist to the wrist of the accused at all times. The guards would work on rotation, so over two years, Paul would have met a great number of them. Biblical scholar and Scotland minister William Barclay pointed out that these guards would have watched closely how Paul lived, witnessed every conversation he had, and heard him preach the gospel. [12] Paul's imprisonment allowed the good news of Jesus to reach a group of people that had previously been unreachable.

Who does Paul say knows that his imprisonment is for Christ? (v. 13)

- According to the previous verse, (v. 12) Paul's imprisonment has served to do what?

- Not only did the Roman army now have access to hear the gospel, but what else did Paul's imprisonment cause? (v. 14)

Sometimes what looks to us like confinement might be the means God uses to advance His Kingdom in amazing ways.

- What does Isaiah 55:8-9 remind us about God?

- What does God's Word tell us in 2 Corinthians 12:10?

In ...orinthians 11:1, Paul tells us to imitate him as he imitates Christ. Let's look at how we ...ght imitate Paul in today's reading.

- In what ways might you be able to advance the gospel because of your unique situation or sufferings?

- Who might be influenced by watching how you walk through daily life?

Philippians 1:15-18a

ADVANCING THE GOSPEL IS NOT A COMPETITION.

Yesterday we learned that Paul's imprisonment was helping advance the gospel. One way this took place is that Christians were watching Paul and becoming *"much more bold to speak the word without fear"* (Philippians 1:14). As we jump into today's reading, this is the group of people referred to in verse 15 with the word "some." The people who were becoming bolder in sharing Christ did so from two different motives.

- According to Philippians 1:15, what were the two groupings of people preaching Christ?

First, let's discuss what these two groups had in common. Both of these were Christian peoples. They preached the true gospel, which is Jesus Christ, salvation through His death on the cross and His bodily resurrection. There wasn't any group that was teaching false doctrine, like a wolf in sheep's clothing. (Matthew 7:15) Paul spoke out adamantly against any attempt to lead people away from the true gospel. So both groups were truly *"preach[ing] Christ"* (Philippians 1:15).

- If their message was the same, what then was the difference between the two groups?

were some people who did not like Paul. Perhaps they dismissed him because of his poor speaking abilities. [13] (1 Corinthians 2:1) Maybe they saw his constant suffering as weakness or disfavor from God. Whatever their reasons, they certainly thought they could do better. And an unhealthy spirit of competition led to rivalry and envy. In his commentary on Philippians, Bible scholar G.W. Hanson said, "The envious begrudge the successes of their opponents and celebrate their misfortunes. The envious person works to harm and ruin the object of envy. Readers of Paul today will observe that envy and rivalry are too often characteristic of preachers of Christ in our competitive churches." [14]

- Have you seen this to be true today, not just in preachers of churches, but in ministry and amongst Christians in general? How about in your own personal relationships? Take a moment to pray, asking God to protect us from rivalry and envy.

Not everyone was selfish in preaching the gospel.

- What words are used to describe those with pure motives?

- To get an even fuller description of this group, take the words used to describe the other side (envy, rivalry, selfish ambition, insincere, attempting to afflict others) and write the **opposite** of these words.

Competition that leads to envy and rivalry has been a human condition since the beginning. Think Cain and Abel. (Genesis 4:1-8) And this instance in Philippians is not the first time Paul has had to deal with this kind of thinking creeping into the Church.

- Read 1 Corinthians 3:3-9. Which two people were Christians trying to put into competition against each other, to gain more "followers"?

- What was Paul's response to this? (1 Corinthians 3:9)

- And what is Paul's attitude toward the competitive spirit in Philippians 1:18?

William Barclay writes, "Paul knew nothing of personal jealousy or of personal resentment. As long as Jesus Christ was preached, he did not care who received the credit and the honour. He did not care what other preachers said about him, or how unfriendly they were to him, or how contemptuous they were of him, or how they tried to go one better and outdo him. All that mattered was that Christ was preached." [15]

- In what areas of your life might an unhealthy competitive spirit be creeping in, and how might you refocus on the main objective today?

Weekend Reflections

For this study, we are going to use the weekends to "go on assignment." Our mission? To put friendship in action.

This week, we studied the opening of the letter to the Philippians. Paul was so thankful for the friends he had in Philippi. Thinking about them filled him with joy, and he wanted them to know it.

This weekend, take a moment to think of the people God has put into your life who fill you with joy. How can you let them know it? A letter, a call, a funny video? Buy them coffee, make them a meal or send them something "just because"? Go for a walk, reminisce over lunch or plan something fun? How can you love them well, using your knowledge of them and discernment, this week?

Let's thank God for the gift of friends and ask Him to show us how to be a friend today as well.

Prayer

Father God, thank You for godly friendships. You created us for community. You don't desire us to be in competition with each other. Instead, You want our relationships to be filled with love and joy in Christ. Show each of us who we can reach out to today to spread Your love. In Jesus' name, amen.

WEEK 2

"*I press on toward the goal
for the prize of the upward call
of God in Christ Jesus.*"

Philippians 3:14

Philippians 1:18b-26

TO LIVE IS CHRIST, TO DIE IS GAIN.

To begin this week, take a moment to highlight every time you see the word "rejoice" or "joy" in today's reading.

There will be three. (verses 18 and 25)

- Read Philippians 1:18b in the NIV translation, and fill in the blank:

  "... Yes, and I will _____ to rejoice ..."

No matter the circumstances, Paul found a reason to rejoice. This type of rejoicing is not sentimental gush or fickle emotion.

- Fill in the blank for the first part of Philippians 1:19. (We will go back to using ESV now.)

  "... for I _____

  _____ ... "

As G.W. Hanson says it, "[Paul's] joy was based on knowledge."[16] It was the knowledge that everything he went through would turn out for his *"deliverance"* (Philippians 1:19). Scholars are not unified on whether this means deliverance from prison or deliverance in terms of eternity. But Paul was sure he would receive deliverance. In the same way, we often do not know if we will be relieved of the struggles we face in this life or the next (eternal life). But we can know that we will one day see relief.

- Knowing deliverance was coming gave Paul an eager expectation and a hope that would not disappoint. How might the assurance of deliverance, whether in this life or in eternal life, give us hope and a reason to rejoice as well?

Backing up just a little, Paul stated that he knew this deliverance would turn out through two means.

- According to Philippians 1:19, deliverance is through 1) "_____ _____"

  and 2) the help of "____ _____ ___ _____ _____"

- Fill in the blanks for Philippians 1:21, *"For to me, ____ _____ is _____ ..."*

  This means to fully live every moment, every breath, for Christ.

- Fill in the end of Philippians 1:21 *"and ___ _____ is _____."*
Pastor Dan Hamel once said, *"In the modern world, we talk about death as if it were the ultimate tragedy. The ultimate tragedy is not that someone dies, but that Jesus not be **known and loved by all**."* [17] How might Christians live differently than the rest of the world when it comes to matters of both life and death?

Life in Paul's world meant encouraging the church, sharing Christ and making His name great. To die meant an eternal life in the presence of Christ Himself.

- According to verses 22-24, how did Paul feel about those two options?

According to William Barclay, "The word he uses is senechomai, the word which would be used of a traveler in a narrow passage, with a wall of rock on either side, unable to turn off in any direction and able only to go straight on. For himself, he wanted to depart and to be with Christ; for the sake of his friends ... he wanted to be left in this life." What makes this word, and it's meaning, so appropriate is that ultimately, "the choice is not [Paul's] but God's." [18]

- What are we reminded of in Lamentations 3:25-26?

Paul knew that if remaining alive and encouraging the Church was the thing that would bring Christ the most glory, then that is exactly what would happen. God would do what was best. He could be trusted.

- In what areas or relationships do you need to trust God's good plan and timing?

Philippians 1:27-28a

TOGETHER, WE CAN LIVE A LIFE WORTHY OF THE GOSPEL.

Today's reading begins with an interesting phrase. It says *"let your manner of life be worthy ..."* (Philippians 1:27). This phrase in Greek is one word, politeuesthe, which more closely translates to "behave as citizens." [19] The people of Philippi prided themselves on the fact that they were also considered Roman citizens. Roman citizenship came with all kinds of benefits and privileges. In turn, the people of Philippi wanted to imitate the Romans in every way, such as how they dressed, spoke and thought.

- According to Philippians 1:27, we are to behave like citizens of the what?

To live a life worthy of the gospel of Christ means as Christians we live differently. We have a higher standard.

- What might it look like to live like this, as citizens of heaven?
  (See 1 John 3:18 for an example.)

We may have many "citizenships," and affiliations. Maybe you're American. Or a farmer. Or a member of a club.

- Write the "citizenships" you have (country, state, city, schools, clubs, denomination). Later in Philippians 3:20 we will learn how *"our citizenship is in heaven."* At the top of your list, write the citizenship that is most important to you.

- Do you have any relationships with people who have a common citizenship in heaven, but who differ in other affiliations? Do you feel that is important? Why or why not?

Our citizenship in heaven is an honor, and that makes us live differently. We want to look and live like Jesus. Paul reminded them to live this way whether he was there to see them, or no one was watching.

- Use a dictionary to find a definition for the word "integrity." How does that relate to Paul's words to *"stand firm"* whether he was there or not?

Standing firm and living to the high standard of the gospel of Christ is not always easy. But we are given a clue in verse 27 that helps.

- Fill in the blank:

"*That ... I may hear of you that you are standing firm in* _____ *spirit, with* _____

mind striving _____ _____ _____*for the faith of the gospel*"

(Philippians 1:27).

We were not meant to do this Christian walk alone. We do it side by side. **Together.** There needs to be unity in the church.

Do you feel this describes Christians today? Why or why not?

Finally, we are told to be *"not frightened in anything by your opponents"* (Philippians 1:28).

- One of the things that should unite us as Christians is our common enemy. Who is this enemy according to Ephesians 6:12?

- I had a teacher who loved to say, "There's safety in numbers." Why might unity help us to not be frightened?

For

to me

to live

is Christ,

and

to die

is gain.

Philippians 1:21

Philippians 1:28b-30

BOTH FAITH AND SUFFERING ARE GIFTS FROM GOD.

Today we will start in the middle of Philippians 1:28. The first sentence starts with the word "this." Let's take a quick look back to see what "this" is referring to.

- In verse 27, Paul said he wanted to hear that the church was standing how?

- In verse 28, Paul said he wanted to hear that the church was not what?

So the word "this" in verse 28 is the unmoved church. [20] It is unified and courageous. When the church looks like this, it is a clear sign to our opponents of their *"destruction"* (Philippians 1:28). When a body of people all agree on the same message, stand firm in that conviction, and are unafraid to face opposition, it gets the attention of those around.

- According to verse 28, the message of the gospel of Christ will be a sign, showing the destruction of those opposed to Him, but also the salvation of those who believe. Both final destruction and salvation will ultimately be from Who?

Verse 29 uses the phrase *"it has been **granted** to you ..."* This is an interesting word choice. The word granted carries the idea of having been "gifted." God has "gifted" us with two things:

- Fill in the blank:

  "For it has been granted to you that for the sake of Christ you should not only

  _____ *in him but also* _____ *for his sake ..." (Philippians 1:29).*

- What does it mean that our faith is a gift from God? (Hint: You don't earn a gift.)

- The second part of this statement is even more mind boggling. According to this verse, even the sufferings of the Church are a gift. [21] Do you view suffering as a gift? Why or why not?

In verse 30, Paul goes on to explain he is speaking of a certain kind of suffering. It is the kind of suffering he has been going through himself. It is specifically suffering for the sake of Jesus.

- Recall how Paul responded to this suffering (see verse 18).

- Read Luke 6:22-23. How does Jesus tell us to respond when people hate us, exclude us, insult us or reject us, because of Him?

- Read 1 Peter 4:12-13. How does Peter tell us to respond to sufferings in Christ?

- Are you prepared to experience hardships for the sake of the gospel? Will you respond in joy?

Philippians 2:1-4

BECAUSE OF CHRIST, WE CAN LEARN UNITY AND HUMILITY.

In the previous days, we heard the call to live a life *"worthy of the gospel of Christ"* (Philippians 1:27). Today we will examine further what it looks like to live this life and the motivations behind it.

Philippians 2:1 gives us four different motivations for what the Word is about to tell us about unity and humility. Let's fill in each motivation and then look at how Bible scholar Eugene Peterson paraphrased each one in *The Message* (**bolded**). [22]

- *"So if there is any _____ in _____."*

    Or you might say, ***"If you've gotten anything at all out of following Christ ..."***

- *"... any _____ from _____ ..."*

    Or ***"... if his love has made any difference in your life ..."***

- *"... any _____ in the _____ ..."*

    Or ***"... if being in a community of the Spirit means anything to you ..."***

- *"... any _____ and _____ ..."*

    Or ***"...if you have a heart, if you care ..."***

Have you gotten anything at all out of following Christ? Has His love made any difference in your life? Does being in a community of the Spirit mean anything to you? Do you have a heart for others and care about them?

If you can answer "yes" to any of these questions, then you can take what you have so graciously been given through Christ and spill it over onto others. Paul gives the Philippians some specific ways, but before we get into those …

- Highlight the word "joy" in Philippians 2:2.

Now let's look into what exactly we do with all that Christ has given us. The first focus is on **unity.**

- According to Philippians 2:2, what kind of mind and love should we have?

- According to G. W. Hanson, "Paul is not squelching human creativity nor is he prohibiting personal diversity. He is calling his friends to 'seek the same goal with a like mind.'" [23] Is it possible to be both diverse and united? (See Revelation 7:9-10 for an example.)

- From what we have studied so far, what is this same goal we share?

The second focus is on **humility**. In God's Word, humility is not so much what you think about yourself, but more about how you treat other people.

- According to verse 3, what do we need to try to avoid?

- What instead does humility "count"?

- It is our nature to look after our own interests ... but, in verse 4, God's Word tells us to also do what?

This kind of humility puts relationships first. It stops to help others get ahead. It promotes others, even if it personally costs us. In the ancient Roman world, humility was not a virtue to be sought after. In fact, it was "despicable." [24] It was seen as a weakness.

- How would you say our culture today views humility?

Tomorrow we will study the ultimate example in humility, and why it is so important to the Christian life. But for today, let's end with a couple of thoughts.

- According to Pastor Dan Hamel, "Paul's logic is clear: in order for the Philippians to live a life worthy of the gospel they must be united, and in order for the Philippians to be united they must treat each other better than they treat themselves." [25] In what ways are humility and unity tied together?

- How are you doing in the areas of unity and humility toward others? Why might biblical humility be especially important in challenging relationships?

Philippians 2:5-11

CHRIST HUMBLED HIMSELF TO THE POINT OF DEATH ON A CROSS.

Today's passage is rich and deep, filled with theology and the beauty of the gospel message. In fact, William Barclay wrote, "In many ways, this is the greatest and most moving passage Paul ever wrote about Jesus." [26] Yesterday, we talked about unity and humility. These can feel like seemingly impossible tasks. How do we accomplish such a mission? Luckily, we are given some insight. Paul says, *"Have this mind among yourselves ..."* In other words, "remember this!" And what are we to remember? Christ Jesus. The only way we live changed, better lives is to think on Jesus. Let's study Christ ...

- Philippians 2:6 says Jesus was in the form of Who?
  This means He was a member of the Godhead. He was fully God.

- The verse goes on to say that Jesus *"did not count* _____ *a thing to be grasped ..."* (Philippians 2:6). This likely has two meanings: First, Jesus didn't have to "grasp" at equality with God because He already had it. Second, Jesus did not "grasp" or hold tight to His equality with God; instead, He laid it down.

- Jesus was fully God, yet the next verse says He *"* _____ *himself ..."* (Philippians 2:7). This word literally means to "pour out until nothing is left inside." This does not mean that Christ became any less "God." Rather, He poured out the rights that were His as King of the universe. [27]

- Verses 7 and 8 tells us that Jesus then took on a new form. What is this new form?

- Fill in (and highlight) the following key phrase:
  "And being found in human form, _____ _____ _____" (Philippians 2:8).

- If leaving heaven and becoming human were not humbling enough, Christ went even further. He became obedient to the point of what?

- What kind of death?

- Take a moment to think about Jesus. Think of the humility He demonstrated. Are you living like Jesus in your relationships?

Humility does not come naturally. It is hard. But we can grow in this area by keeping our eyes fixed on Jesus and remembering what He went through for us. It also helps knowing the rest of the story ...

Humility does not come naturally. It is hard. But we can grow in this area by keeping our eyes fixed on Jesus and remembering what He went through for us. It also helps knowing the rest of the story ...

- Jesus, fully God, also became fully man, and fully died a humiliating death on a cross. "Therefore," verse 9 says, God has done what?

- Philippians 2:10 says that at the name of Jesus, what will happen?

- Verse 11 says that every tongue will do what?

- What did Jesus say in Luke 14:11?

God Is In The Details

Philippians 2:10-11 says, "... so that **at the name of Jesus**, every knee should bow, in heaven and on earth and under the earth, and every tongue confess that **Jesus Christ is Lord**, to the glory of God the Father." (Philippians 2:10-11, emphasis added)

You may have heard this verse before and understood it's meaning. But did you know that this cleverly crafted sentence struck a note with two different people groups and the very different issues they were facing in regard to Jesus? The subtle details of these verses make them even more rich!

What you heard if you were Jewish...

Anyone who had been taught from the Jewish scriptures would have known Isaiah 45:21-23. It says, *"And there is no other god besides me, a righteous God and a Savior; there is none besides me. Turn to me and be saved, all the ends of the earth! For I am God, and there is no other. ... 'To me every knee shall bow, every tongue shall swear allegiance.'"* Jews understood this to mean there is only one God, and **He** would be the Savior. **To God Himself**, every knee would bow and every tongue would swear allegiance.

In Philippians 2:10-11, Paul quotes from Isaiah 45:23, with just a small change. Instead of *"To me"* (me being God), he adds *"at the name of Jesus."* What Paul said would have been absolutely mind-blowing to them, and they would have heard it loud and clear:

"Jesus is God."

What you heard if you were gentile...

At this time in history, Rome ruled the land. And the Roman Emperor Caesar was more than a leader. In Roman mythology, Jupiter and other gods had given divine rights to Caesar. [8] In essence, Caesar was god. He was lord. Everyone was reminded of that fact, especially in a Roman colony like Philippi.

What Paul said in Philippians 2:10-11 would have also been extreme to gentiles. In the face of the Roman government, this verse says that one day every knee and every tongue, everywhere in the entire world, will one day bow and confess ... not that Caesar is lord ... but that ...

"Jesus is Lord."

Which makes Jesus way more important and far greater than the most powerful man or "god" they could imagine.

Jews believed only in worshipping God. Paul said Jesus is God.

Gentile Romans believed in allegiance to Caesar, the lord. Paul said Jesus is Lord.

One small verse in Philippians, but it carried enormous meaning to all who heard it.

Weekend Reflections

This week, we studied how suffering for Christ is a cause for joy. We talked about humility and what it looks like, specifically by looking at just how far Jesus humbled Himself for us.

This weekend, our assignment is to put friendship into action through humility. Who is someone you can serve? Sometimes serving is messy or inconvenient. It tends to rub against our selfish nature. Remind yourself of how Jesus said He came "not to be served but to serve" (Matthew 20:28). What is a way you can "count others more significant than yourselves" (Philippians 2:3) today?

Being humble helps us look a little more like Jesus, and there is no greater friend than Him!

Prayer

God, thank You for demonstrating ultimate humility. You left heaven and died on a cross for me. Help me walk in humility today, loving others like You love me. Please show me where I can serve. In Jesus' name, amen.

WEEK 3

"Therefore, my brothers, whom I love and long for, my joy and crown, stand firm thus in the Lord, my beloved."

Philippians 3:14

Philippians 2:12-13

GOD ENABLES US TO WALK OUT OUR SALVATION.

Last week, we studied Christ and the sacrifice He made for us. It was the ultimate demonstration of humility. As followers of Christ, we are united under Him and want to be like Him in humility as well. Today we'll explore even deeper what our salvation in Christ looks like.

But to begin, let's touch on a moment of friendship in this letter. Paul loves the people of Philippi.

- What term of endearment does he call his friends in Philippians 2:12?

- Do the people in your life know how much they mean to you? How can you show them today?

Paul commends his friends for their obedience and encourages them to do so more and more. He then says an interesting line at the end of verse 12.

- Fill in the blank:
  "... work out your own _____ ... "

In order to fully understand this statement, let's spend some time talking about salvation. This verse is **not** saying *"work for your salvation."* Ephesians 2:8-9 tells us that salvation is not by works. So what does it mean to "work out" your salvation? Well, let's take a look at the three categories of salvation. I particularly like how Jen Wilkin worded them as freedom from the 3 P's of sin — penalty, power and presence. [28]

JUSTIFICATION

When we confess our sin and need for Jesus, we are "justified" or forgiven of our sins. At that moment, we are free from sin's **penalty**, which is eternal death. Once we are justified, we never need to be re-justified.

- What does Romans 8:1-2 teach us about salvation (by justification)?

- Write a few thoughts about the day of your justification.

SANCTIFICATION

Once God's grace is permanently set upon us, we begin an ongoing process of being set free from sin's **power**. We have the Holy Spirit to help us choose righteousness. Yes, we will still sin, but over time, we learn to increasingly choose holiness. (2 Peter 1:8)

- What does 2 Corinthians 4:16 teach us about salvation (in sanctification)?

- How does Philippians 2:12 fit into the category of sanctification?

GLORIFICATION

At the end of our life, or when Jesus returns, because of our justification, we will receive glorification. We will be in the presence of God! Then we will be free from sin's **presence**. No more will we have sin in our hearts and minds. It will be gone forever.

Jen Wilkin sums it up like this: "Be assured of your justification. It *was*. One day, you were freed fully from the penalty of sin. Be patient with your sanctification. It *is*. Each day, you are being freed increasingly from the power of sin. Be eager for your glorification. *It is to come*. One day, you will be freed finally from the presence of sin." [29]

- What stood out to you in studying the three categories of salvation?

Philippians 2:12-13 refers to our sanctification. It is the daily workings of becoming more like Christ.

- According to verse 12, we should work out our salvation with what attitude?

- Fear and trembling sound scary. But biblical fear means "reverence." And trembling can also be translated as "sincere loyalty." [30] How do these expanded definitions help you understand verse 12?

The key to all of this is found in verse 13.

- According to verse 13, who does the work of sanctification in our lives?

- Therefore, who gets the glory for any change in us, any good choices we make, right words we say, nice things we do, etc.?

Philippians 2:14-18

WE CAN SHINE AS LIGHTS IN THE WORLD.

Today we'll continue to explore how we can be more like Jesus.

- According to Philippians 2:14, we are to do all things without what?

Grumblings are low, threatening or discontented mutterings. Disputing is useless or ill-natured questioning.

- In what way has either of these definitions described your attitude in the past week?

The verse goes on to say that we avoid grumbling and complaining so that we can show ourselves to be true and sincere children of God. As God's children, we look and act different from a *"crooked and twisted generation"* (Philippians 2:15).

- When God's people went out from Egypt and into the wilderness, how were they described in Deuteronomy 32:5?

- What had the people of Israel done, according to Exodus 16:2 and 8?

Complaining is the way of the world. As Christians, we are called to stand out from the world. In fact, Philippians 2:15 says we *"shine as lights in the world."* The NIV translates this as *"shine among them like stars in the sky."* A night sky is dark. In contrast, the light of a star, though billions of miles away, stands out.

- What did Jesus say in Matthew 5:16?

- What did Jesus call Himself in John 8:12?

- Who, then, do we look like when we *"shine as lights in the world"*?

Paul went on to talk about how he wanted to be proud of the church in Philippi. Let's look at the words he used to describe what he had done among them.

- Fill in the blanks for Philippians 2:16-17.

  "... so that in the day of Christ I may be proud that I did not _____ in vain or

  _____ in vain. Even if I am to be _____ _____ as a drink offering upon

  the sacrificial offering of your faith ..."

Sharing the gospel and loving and ministering to God's people isn't easy. It requires all parts of us. We don't walk; we **run** toward helping people. We don't just think; we **labor** and we put our words into action. We don't hold anything back. We **pour** ourselves out.

- Highlight the word "rejoice" in verses 17 and 18 (there are two).

For Paul, joy came from the work he put into the Philippian church. There is joy to be found in loving other people. Paul also said that the Philippians should have joy, too. There is also joy in having people who nurture our souls and love us well.

- Take a moment to apply today's reading to your life. Is your work and service in your relationships with others characterized more by grumbling or joy? How do you know?

Philippians 2:19-24

TIMOTHY WAS A GENUINE SERVANT OF THE GOSPEL.

To begin today, let's get a good overarching idea of today's reading.

- Who does Paul name specifically, and what was his character?

By following the accounts of Paul's missionary journeys in Acts, and in reading his letters throughout the New Testament, we learn a little about Timothy's service to both Paul and the Church. We know he was with Paul in Philippi, Thessalonica, Berea, Corinth, Ephesus and when Paul was imprisoned in Rome. Timothy was associated with Paul in writing 1 and 2 Thessalonians, 2 Corinthians, Colossians and Philippians. Also, in Romans, it is mentioned that Timothy sends his greetings. When Paul needed a message delivered, he often sent Timothy, which leads us to believe that Timothy traveled back to places like Thessalonica, Corinth and Philippi. We may not think often about Timothy, but he was a foundational part of the early church. William Barclay says Timothy serves as an example "of all those who are quite content with second place, as long as they can serve." [31]

- What do we learn about service from Timothy's example?

Let's take a look at the friendship shared between Paul and Timothy.

- In Philippians 2:20, Paul said, *"For I have ..."* what?

- In verse 22, Paul compared their relationship to that of what two people?

- In what ways might close friendships become like family?

Timothy was trusted to deliver the message and check on the church because he was known to be "genuinely concerned" for others (Philippians 2:20).

- Use a dictionary to define the word "genuine."

- In Philippians 2:21, Paul speaks of other helpers when he says ...

  "For they all seek _____ _____ _____, not those of Jesus Christ."

- This does not mean that everyone else in the world was not genuine. Rather, it is emphasizing that sincere servants, even within the church, are rare. Matthew Henry calls self-seeking "very common among Christians and ministers" and goes on to say "Many prefer their own credit, ease, and safety, before truth, holiness, and duty, the things of their own pleasure and reputation before the things of Christ's kingdom..." [32] Do you agree or disagree with this view and why?

Today's section of reading begins and ends with a similar phrase. Let's wrap up by taking a look at this.

- Philippians 2:19, *"I hope _____ _____ _____ _____ to ..."*

- Philippians 2:24, *"I trust _____ _____ _____ that ..."*

- What do we learn from James 4:13-15?

Paul knew his situation in prison was unpredictable. He did not know whether he would live to preach, or die a martyr's death. We learned in Philippians 1:21 that he was ready for either. He was not worried. And he went ahead and made plans for the future … but always while realizing that God had the final say.

- Do you tend to build your future plans with concrete, or do you make plans that allow for the Holy Spirit's guidance and movement along the way?

How does Proverbs 16:9 apply here?

Philippians 2:25-30

EPAPHRODITUS RISKED HIS LIFE FOR THE WORK OF CHRIST.

Yesterday, we looked at the life of Timothy and his role in assisting Paul. Today, we'll study another friend of Paul and the church at Philippi.

- What is the name of the man sent to Paul in Philippians 2:25?

- According to this same verse, why did the Philippians send him?

When the church at Philippi heard that Paul was in prison, they were moved to do something to help. While they put together a monetary gift of some sort, they also made another big sacrifice. They decided to send the gift with Epaphroditus, with the intention that he would stay in Rome and help Paul. [33] This was a big ask. Epaphroditus was going to move to Rome to become the personal assistant to a man whose trial could end in the death penalty. However, something interrupted Epaphroditus' service to Paul.

- What happened to Epaphroditus when he got to Rome? (verse 27)

Perhaps it was the notorious Roman fever that afflicted Epaphroditus. It would often sweep through the city of Rome like a plague. Whatever it was, it almost cost Epaphroditus his life. What had been meant to be a blessing to Paul could now be mistaken as a burden. As Steven Runge says it, "Imagine the embarrassment of sending a highly expected gift only to have it arrive broken or spoiled." [34]

- Have you ever given a gift or done something with good intentions, only for it to go awry? How did you feel?

Paul was "returning" his gift. He was sending Epaphroditus back home. But he did not want the church to be embarrassed. And he certainly did not want them thinking that Epaphroditus had failed. Let's look at the carefully crafted words Paul uses to describe Epaphroditus.

- In Philippians 2:25, Paul calls Epaphroditus...

  "*my* _____ ..." (meaning my equal, my family)

  "*and* _____ _____ ..." (like-minded in mission)

  "*and* _____ _____ ..." (partners in danger)

- He goes on to call Epaphroditus...

    "your _____ *"* (Paul uses the Greek word apostolos, which means anyone

    who is sent out on an errand. But in Christian circles it also carried the honor of being

    like the apostles.) *"and* _____ *to my need..."* (Paul uses the Greek word
    leitourgos, which was a magnificent word in secular Greek. It was the word used for men
    who loved their city so much, they became benefactors and gave of their own resources to
    build it up.)

William Barclay says, "Paul takes the great Christian word apostolos and the great Greek word *leitourgos*, and applies them to *Epaphroditus*. 'Give a man like that a welcome home', he says. 'Hold him in honour, for he risked his life for Christ.' Paul is making it easy for Epaphroditus to go home." [35]

- What was Paul's own situation again? (Philippians 1:13)

- Yet his focus is not on his own situation. What made Paul anxious in Philippians 2:28?

- What does this teach us about the focus of our cares and concerns?

Let's look at one more lesson from today's reading.

- According to verse 30, Epaphroditus had nearly died and had risked his life for what?

- What did Jesus say were the two greatest commandments in Matthew 22:37-39?

- The Faithlife Study Bible says, "Believers who take risks and endure suffering for the sake of others and for the gospel are worthy of great respect." [36] When was the last time you took a risk to love and serve both God and others?

Philippians 3:1-3

OUR CONFIDENCE IS IN CHRIST JESUS.

To begin today, let's be reminded of one of the major themes of Philippians.

- Highlight the word "rejoice" in Philippians 3:1.

Paul tells the Philippians he is going to *"write the same things"* to them. In other words, he is going to remind them of something they had already been taught. We all need reminders. Often God will put a message in front of us repeatedly to get our attention and help it sink in.

- Pastor Dan Hamel once asked this question. "Over the past 3 months, what themes has God repeatedly placed before you through the sermons you have heard, the conversations you have had, and the passages of Scripture you have read? What is God trying to **communicate to you?**" [37] Take a moment to answer this question for yourself.

The message Paul wants to remind his friends at Philippi of has to do with false teachers. There was a group of people, often called Judaizers, [38] who were teaching the new gentile Christians that they needed to also obey the Torah, and essentially become Jewish, if they were also to follow Christ. This teaching infuriated Paul and he adamantly taught against it his entire life. Let's look at the words used in today's reading.

- Philippians 3:2 says, *"Look out for the _____ ..."*
  There is a Jewish Rabbinic saying: "The nations of the world are like dogs." [39] To Jews, dogs were low life. They were dirty scavengers who transmitted disease. And because gentiles were seen as "unclean," many Jews had taken to calling them "dogs." Here, Paul flips it and says the real "dogs" are these Jewish false teachers.

- This verse goes on to say, *"... look out for the evildoers, look out for those who _____ the _____"* (Philippians 3:2). This was Paul's strong descriptive language to refer to circumcision.

Let's take a moment to discuss circumcision.

- God gave the command to Abraham in Genesis 17:11. It was to be a sign of what?

Circumcision under the old covenant was the physical sign that you belonged to God. But things changed when Jesus came and established a new covenant.

- Read Galatians 5:2-6. Circumcision is tied to the old law. And the old law couldn't save us. According to Galatians 5:6, under Christ, what is the value of circumcision?

- In that same verse, what is the only thing that counts? (or ... what is our new outward "sign" that we belong to God?)

Philippians 3:3 says that "we are the circumcision."

- This "we" means the Church — a group of people who do what three things (according to verse 3)?

1.

2.

3.

- The "flesh" is anything outside of Christ. Knowing this, where, then, is our confidence?

Weekend Reflections

This week, we started with a good reminder. We do not run around, accomplishing "good works" to be justified before God. When we accepted Jesus' free gift of salvation, we were fully forgiven and saved. Not because of what we had done or will do, but because of Jesus and His love. Now we go out doing good and spreading joy and friendship because we want to be more like Christ.

We looked at two different men this week who Paul sets up as an example for us. Timothy was a genuine, selfless servant. In no way did he desire attention or recognition for all that he did. Epaphroditus literally risked his life in order to serve. And even though his plan didn't go as expected, he was still honored for trying.

Our assignment for this weekend is to try serving in secret. Is there something you can do anonymously? A gift you can give, a service you can provide, an encouraging word? Can you try this not only with those you know well, but maybe with someone who feels against you? Even if it feels risky, or you don't know how it will be received, take a step of faith and let God guide you.

Sometimes quiet acts of friendship are the most powerful, because all the credit and glory goes to God!

Prayer

Father God, how can I serve in secret this weekend? Show me what You want me to do. I pray all the glory and credit and recognition go to You, Lord! In Jesus' name, amen.

WEEK 4

"*Rejoice in the Lord always; again I will say, rejoice.*"

Philippians 4:4

Philippians 3:4-7

OUR IDENTITY IS NOT IN THIS WORLD.

In the previous reading, we looked at Paul's rejection of Judaizers. These were Jewish people who went around telling gentiles they must become "Jewish" (and be circumcised according to the Torah) if they wanted to follow Jesus. Today, we'll see Paul's personal Jewish history. If anyone could claim to be the "perfect" Jew, it was Paul.

- According to Philippians 3:5, Paul was "_____ *on the* _____ *day* ..."

- What did the law teach in Leviticus 12:3?

- He was a *"Hebrew of* _____*."* This meant both of his parents were true-blooded Hebrews.

- As to the law, Paul was a what?

- Pharisees were religious leaders who were particularly devoted to keeping the law to the letter. Paul wasn't just any Pharisee, either. According to Acts 22:3, he studied under a well-known teacher named Gamaliel. What does Galatians 1:14 also tell us about Paul and his studies as a Pharisee?

- Philippians 3:6 goes on to say that Paul was a "_____ *of the church ...*" He directly and violently opposed anyone against the Jewish way of life.

- He ends his list with *"as to righteousness under the law, _____."* Paul was not saying he was sinless. Rather, he had done everything required under the law. If the law could have saved him, he would have been the prime member to receive it.

If there was anyone who had Jewish bragging rights, it was Paul. He had the pedigree, reputation, occupation, schooling, connections, you name it.

- Yet what does he say in Philippians 3:7?

Galatians 2:16 tells us "a person is not justified by works of the law but through faith in Jesus Christ." The truth is, the law couldn't save Paul, just as good works cannot save us. Only Jesus can save. Everything else the world says is "good" is like rubbish compared to Jesus.

- What does Ephesians 2:8-9 remind us?

As Christians, our identity isn't tied to this world. Who we are isn't based on our family names, our looks, our finances, our occupations, our IQ levels, our schooling, our fitness abilities, our social connections … the list goes on. These things might matter to the world, but we count them as loss. Who we are is based on Whose we are. And we belong to Jesus.

- Look at the chart entitled "My Identity" on the next page. On the top half of the chart, write the worldly standards you may have been using to measure your identity. Whether, like Paul, you have a background to brag about, or if you have parts you wish weren't there, but still feel defined by, put them all down in this list. We will come back to this tomorrow.

My Identity

WORLD'S STANDARDS/RELIGIOUS STANDARDS
REAL WORTH

One final note for today. Notice the power of personal testimony. Paul willingly shared his personal story. He used it all to show the power of Jesus.

- What part of your story can you share to show others what God has done in your life?

Philippians 3:8-11

OUR SURPASSING WORTH IS IN KNOWING CHRIST.

Yesterday, we looked at false teachers who had been telling new Christians they had to live like Jews, obeying Old Testament law and ways, particularly circumcision. Paul used his own life's story to show how this was foolish. He had every Jewish achievement imaginable, but he said he counted them as loss because they were worth nothing compared to Jesus. In fact, there is a very specific word used to describe these worldly measures.

- In Philippians 3:8, it says *"... I have suffered the loss of all things and count them as ... "* what?

The word "rubbish," *skubalon* in Greek, was a word used to describe excrement and trash that had been thrown out, often for dogs to forage through. [40] An interesting depiction.

- Who had Paul called "dogs" in Philippians 3:2?

- What was he now referring to as rubbish?

Today's section also says we do not have a righteousness of our own that comes from the law. (v. 9)

- What does Romans 3:10 say?

- Go back to the list you made yesterday in the My Identity Chart. Sometimes, it is not just the world's standards we try to live up to. Sometimes, we (or others) have set for ourselves religious standards that are also incorrect. Have you ever done what the Bible refers to as "good works" because you thought it would make God love or accept you? Write those down in this section as well.

- There is no amount of righteousness in our own works that brings us into right standing before God. And our measure of worth isn't defined by worldly standards. On your chart, in big, bold letters, write over your list the word "RUBBISH." These things are rubbish if we place any confidence in them.

We have talked about what is "loss" and "rubbish." Now let's look at what is of "surpassing worth." (Philippians 3:8)

- Surpassing worth means "of the highest value." According to verse 8, what is of greatest value?

- According to verses 8-9, everything else is rubbish in order that we might have what two things?

- And where is our righteousness found? (v. 9)

- In your Identity Chart, under "Real Worth" write the following: Knowing Christ. Gaining Christ. Being in Christ. After each one, circle the word "Christ." What stands out to you in doing this chart?

- How might knowing your true identity also affect your relationships with others?

There are two specific areas of knowing Christ that are emphasized in verses 10-11.

- The first is to know the power of His what?

- The second is to share in His what?

Christ suffered to the point of death so that we could have life. His very resurrection is the proof of His power and triumph over sin and death. And when we know, gain and live in Christ, we share in both His suffering and His power.

- No matter what we face today, we can trust that in Christ, someday we will attain what? (v. 11)

Philippians 3:12-16

WE PRESS ON TOWARD THE PRIZE IN CHRIST.

Today's section of Scripture begins with a confession.

- Paul readily admits that he is not what? (Philippians 3:12)

The Greek word for "perfect," *teleios* means "being perfected, being completed or reaching a goal." We are reminded that once we become a Christ-follower, this does not mean we are done. We are not suddenly perfect. We have not reached our final destination yet. Instead, once we decide to follow Christ, we are now on a journey. We work hard and strive toward holiness — not for salvation.

- Why does Paul say he will continue to strive toward "perfect"? (Philippians 3:12)

- In what ways might that motivation change your behavior?

Philippians 3:15 says, *"Let those of us who are mature think this way ..."* The word "mature" can also be translated as "perfect." In fact, it is the same Greek word that was used in verse 12. According to the ESV Study Bible, "Paul is saying, in effect, 'If you are really perfect/mature, you will realize you are not yet perfect/mature!'" [41]

- As you age and mature, do you find this to be true?

In Philippians 3:13, Paul tells us the "one thing" he does. It comes in two parts.

- "... _____ *what lies* _____ ..."

- "... *and* _____ _____ *to what lies* _____ ..."

What lies behind us includes both our past accomplishments and our past failures. These we can forget. Instead, we focus on what is before us. According to William Barclay, the Greek word for "straining forward," *epekteinomenos,* "is very vivid and is used of a racer going hard for the finishing line. It describes someone with eyes for nothing but the goal. It describes the person who is going flat out for the finish." [42]

- According to verse 14, what are we "straining forward" or "pressing on" toward?

Matthew Henry says, "Heaven is the *prize of the high calling;* ... the *prize* we fight for, and run for, and wrestle for, what we aim at in all we do, and what will reward all our pains." [43]

- What makes heaven the ultimate prize? (Matthew 25:34; 1 Peter 1:4; Revelation 21:4)

- How might keeping our focus on heaven affect how we live now?

Finally, today's section ends with some wise words about times when Christians disagree. Paul tells the members of the church at Philippi that if any of them disagree with him, they should do two things.

- According to verse 15, we should ask and trust Whom to reveal the truth to both us and them?

- According to Philippians 3:16, we should *"hold _____ to what we have attained."* In other words, we make sure anything we believe first and foremost holds true to the truth we have been given — the Bible.

- How can you apply these principles the next time you aren't sure you agree with someone?

I have learned in whatever situation I am to be content.

Philippians 4:11

Philippians 3:17-4:1

THERE ARE THOSE WE DO AND DO NOT IMITATE.

To begin, let's look at how our themes of friendship and joy can be seen in today's reading.

- Highlight the word "joy" in Philippians 4:1.

- Now look at the term Paul uses in Philippians 3:17 to describe the recipients of his letter. It's the same term he uses in Philippians 4:1. What does he call them?

- What additional terms of endearment does he use in 4:1?

Friendship

We need people who walk beside us and encourage us. We need people who inspire us to keep *"press[ing] on toward the goal ..."* (Philippians 3:14). We need people in our lives who we love and long for ... people whose very presence helps us *"stand firm"* in the Lord (Philippians 4:1). Pastor Dan Hamel said it this way, "The people you join with in your journey to the cross will have an extremely significant role in your life and faith. An isolated life is both practically ineffective and theologically inconsistent. You won't be transformed in isolation ... You won't be able to accurately reflect the character of God in isolation." [44] In summary, **friendship matters.**

- Read Acts 2:42. The early church was dedicated to the apostles' teaching, to communion, to prayer and to what?

- Are you satisfied with the quality and quantity of spiritual friendships in your life? Why or why not?

Discipleship

Friendship and fellowship are vital parts of the Christian life. The next level of this would be discipleship. A disciple is someone who has been taught or trained. This requires a teacher, and the best teachers lead by example.

- In Philippians 3:17, Paul asks his friends to join in doing what?

- He also says to keep their eyes on who?

The ESV Study Bible says, "Much Christian growth comes through imitation of other Christians." [45] Paul gave the church in Philippi several examples, through Timothy, through Epaphroditus and in himself.

- Who do you look to as a good example for Christian living? What good do you see in them that you wish to imitate?

Bad Influences

Just as important as it is to have good influences in our lives, it is equally important to be on the lookout for the bad. The church in Philippi was given three things to watch out for:

- Philippians 3:19 says that for the enemies of the cross, *"Their end is _____ ..."*

This means they are taking the wrong path. Do not follow them there!

- *"... their god is their _____..."*

  They worship their desires, their passions and their ways. They do what feels good.

- *"... and they glory in their _____ ..."*

  They take pride in things that should embarrass them. They are proud of their sin.

- Where have you seen any of these influences lately ... in the world and in your personal life?

Our Main Influence

- According to Philippians 3:20, our citizenship is where?

This was a huge reminder to the audience of this letter. Philippi was a Roman colony, which was a great source of pride to its citizens. Being a Roman colony allowed them to be considered Roman citizens. This carried all kinds of benefits for a person during this time period (such as massive tax breaks, just to name one!) Because they were so proud to be considered "Roman," they tried to look like and imitate Rome in all they did ... to the point where they looked like a "little Rome."

- In a similar way, how does knowing that our "citizenship" is in heaven help inspire us?

- Who do we imitate first and foremost? (Hint, it is the one we await in verse 20.)

Philippians 4:2-3

IT IS IMPORTANT TO DEAL WITH DISAGREEMENTS.

Today's reading might leave us with questions. Who were Euodia and Syntyche? What was their quarrel about? What work did these women do with Paul to further the gospel? Who is Clement and what role did he play? Unfortunately, we cannot answer these questions definitively. However, we do have much to learn about relationships from this situation.

- Philippians 4:2 tells us that these two women were "entreated" or urged or pleaded with, to do what?

- What was encouraged earlier in Philippians 2:2?

- In today's passage, does Paul give any mention of what the argument was about? Whose side did he choose? (Yes, that is a trick question.)

- How often do you think we might have arguments over things that, in the long run, aren't significant? Can you think of a personal example?

- Yet also notice that Paul did not just say "They'll get over it eventually." It needed to be dealt with. Why might it be important to deal with disagreements instead of ignoring them?

Imagine being called out by name in the Bible. Ouch. It is not pleasant to have to be corrected, and especially in front of a crowd. But notice what else Paul says in verse 3.

- We know these two women argued, but what else do we know about them?

- Why is it important to pair correction with praise?

In regard to these verses, William Barclay said, "It is significant that, when there was a quarrel at Philippi, Paul mobilized the whole resources of the church to mend it. He thought no effort too great to maintain the peace of the church." [46]

- Do we treat disagreements with our fellow brothers and sisters in Christ with the same level of importance? Why or why not?

Paul specifically called on a *"true companion"* (Philippians 4:3) to help mend the peace. It is suggested that the Greek word *sunzugos* can also be a proper name, and may be a specific person. We do not know for certain. What we do know is that someone was asked to intervene, to help the situation.

- Why might it be important to involve the help of a third-party to settle arguments?

- In what ways can you help be a peacemaker to those around you?

Weekend Reflections

This week, we studied how our identity is not defined by this world. Our identity is in Christ. We are His! Therefore, we live life running toward the prize that is heaven. And what a prize it will be! We are citizens of heaven. How good it is to encourage, and be encouraged, as we walk toward heaven together.

This weekend, try slipping a little heaven into your conversations. The other day, as I was brushing my daughter's hair, she told me, "I'm glad there won't be tangles in heaven." Ha! *Yes, and amen.* How can you remind someone of our heavenly home today? Maybe you just pose the question "What are you most looking forward to in heaven?" and see what other people say.

Let's encourage each other, building friendship and spreading joy by thinking about our future home in heaven together.

Prayer

Father, how I look forward to heaven! I cannot wait to sit at Your feet. I cannot wait for an eternity in Your presence. In my mind, I imagine so many things. Yet, I know it will be even more wonderful than that. Help me to encourage a fellow brother or sister today. Help me to remind them of home. In Jesus' name, amen.

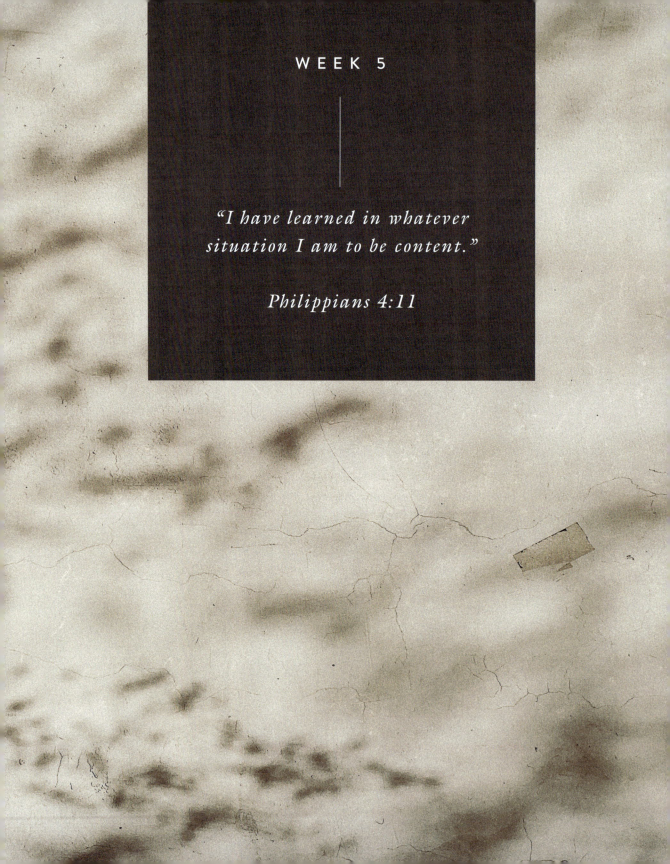

WEEK 5

"*I have learned in whatever situation I am to be content.*"

Philippians 4:11

Philippians 4:4-5

REJOICE IN THE LORD ALWAYS.

Today, we reach the pinnacle of this letter's call to joy.

- Highlight the two instances of the word "rejoice" in Philippians 4:4.

It is important to remember the circumstances in which this letter was written. Paul had been persecuted, shipwrecked, stoned, beaten and was currently in prison awaiting a trial that could end in his execution. The church in Philippi was set in the midst of a hostile people. Jews and Romans alike wanted the Christians extinguished.

- And yet, even in the midst of all of this, what did Paul urge the Christians to do in verse 4?

A joyless Christian should be an oxymoron. The Christian life is a life of joy and hope.

- What is it about the gospel that might inspire hope and optimism?

Let's focus on three specific phrases also used in Philippians 4:4...

- *"Rejoice ____ _____ _____ ..."*
  Our circumstances will not always bring us joy. Nor our jobs or marriages or children or friends. There is only one constant source of joy.

- *"Rejoice in the Lord _____ ..."*
  We do not rejoice because life is always good, but because God is always good.

- *"Rejoice in the Lord always; _____ I will say, _____."*
  Just in case anyone was asking, "Really? Because if you only knew ...," William Barclays writes, "So Paul says: 'I know what I'm saying. I've thought of everything that can possibly happen. And still I say it—Rejoice!'" [47]

- Which of these three phrases sticks out to you and why?

1 Thessalonians 5:16 is a verse with only two words. It says, *"Rejoice always."* Joy defines the Christian life. It is that important.

- What characteristics seem to be present in a person of joy?

- How would you assess your level of joy currently? Why might that be the case?

Philippians 4:5 says, *"Let your reasonableness be known to everyone."* The Greek word *epieikeia*, or "reasonableness" according to the ESV, is a difficult word to translate. Other Bible translations use words like "gentleness" or "patience." Eugene Peterson refers to it as "you're on their side, working with them and not against them." [48] The ESV Study Bible says, "it is the disposition that seeks what is best for everyone and not just for oneself." [49]

- What might this look like in practical terms?

- How might this affect your relationships if this phrase were to describe you?

To rejoice always, and to treat others with a constant state of gentleness and care is certainly not easy. Verse 5 ends with an encouraging note ...

- Philippians 4:5: *"The Lord is ___ _____."*

- What does Psalm 145:18 remind us?

- The Lord is at hand, ready to help us. In fact, if we want to bear the fruits of joy and gentleness, there is only one way. According to John 15:5, what is that way?

Philippians 4:6-7

DO NOT BE ANXIOUS ABOUT ANYTHING.

Yesterday, we looked at joy. This was more than a command to "be happy." This was a joy focused on God's goodness, despite current circumstances. Paul wasn't in good circumstances. And the church in Philippi had much to be worried about. Yet Philippians 4:6 gives a clear imperative (or command).

- Philippians 4:6: *"... do not be _____ about _____."*

Jesus gave similar commands to what we read here in Philippians.

- What did Jesus say in Matthew 6:25?

- What about in Matthew 6:34?

Pastor Dan Hamel once said, "Anxiety is rooted in fear of circumstances which we cannot *control* and the future which we cannot *know*." [50]

- What makes you anxious? Does it fall into these categories of "circumstances which we cannot **control**" and "the future which we cannot **know**"?

As Christians, we can look differently at anxiety. One reason is because we know Who is in control, and Who holds the future.

- What does Romans 8:28 teach us about Who is in control?

- What does Isaiah 26:3 remind us when we feel anxious?

Philippians 4:6 goes on to demonstrate how we can help battle anxiety:

- *"... but in everything by _____ and _____ with _____ let your requests be made known to God."*

Eighteenth century Greek scholar Johann Bengel said "Anxiety and prayer (*curare et orare*) are more opposed to each other than fire and water..." [51]

- Do you turn to prayer when you worry? Why or why not?

A vital component of this battle is **thanksgiving**. This does not always come naturally to us. We have to work at it, practice it. Nineteenth century philosopher Ralph Waldo Emerson noted that we must "cultivate the habit of being grateful." [52]

- Take a moment to write five things you are thankful for. Try adding to this list every day this week.

I'm Thankful For ...

1.

2.

3.

4.

5.

Philippians 4:7 goes on to say...

- *"And the peace of God, which _____ ____ _____, ..."*
  Having peace when the rest of the world is worried and anxious certainly won't make sense to everyone.

- *"... will _____ your _____ and your _____ in Christ Jesus."*

The word "guard" is *phrourein* in Greek. It is a military word meaning *"standing on guard,"* like a centurion on duty. Philippi was a garrison town, meaning it would have had Roman sentry constantly about, ready to protect it.

- In what ways is God's peace like a guard for our hearts and minds?

In light of what we have learned today ...

- What is one thing you can do the next time you start to feel anxious?

To any of our friends who suffer with anxiety and depression, we want you to know that the joy and hope of Jesus are not at odds with good counseling and good medical intervention. What a blessing God has given in providing ways to help us ... body, soul and mind.

AND THE PEACE OF GOD,

WHICH SURPASSES

ALL UNDERSTANDING,

WILL GUARD YOUR HEARTS

AND YOUR MINDS

IN CHRIST JESUS.

PHILIPPIANS 4:7

Philippians 4:8-9

THINK ABOUT WHAT IS TRUE AND PRAISEWORTHY.

The average person has more than 30,000 thoughts per day. But here is the real showstopper: Of those thoughts, researchers estimate that a full 70% of them are negative. Jennie Allen, author of *Get Out of Your Head*, wrote, "The greatest spiritual battle of our generation is being fought between our ears."[53]

Within her book, Jennie goes on to describe scientific research that actually confirms, "What we think about, our brains become. What we fixate on is neurologically who we will be. ... Tell me what you're thinking about, in other words, and I'll tell you who you are."[54]

- How would you describe your thought life? Are you surprised by the statistic that 70% of our thoughts are negative? Why or why not?

- What does 2 Corinthians 10:5 tell us to do with our thoughts?

Today's reading is an excellent Scripture to commit to memory. Within Philippians 4:8, we find the types of thoughts that can transform our minds.

- *"Finally, brothers, whatever is _____..."*
  Write a thought that is true.

- *"... whatever is _____..."*
  Write about something that is honorable.

- *"... whatever is _____..."*
  Write something you have seen that is just.

- *"... whatever is _____..."*
  Write about the most recent thing you have seen that is pure.

- *"... whatever is _____..."*
  Write about something lovely in creation.

- *"... whatever is _____..."*
  Write something you have seen lately that you admire.

- *"If there is any _____..."*
  Write about something done that reflects excellence.

- *"... if there is anything _____ of _____..."*
  Write something that makes you want to give praise.

Look at all the words written in the blanks above.

- Who is the only One who fits into all of these categories, and therefore, is truly the One we should keep our minds focused on?

As we mentioned earlier, our thoughts affect who we are. They will affect our choices and our actions. Our thoughts become our "*practice*" (Philippians 4:9).

- According to Philippians 4:9, if we practice these things, what will be with us?

I want to end with one final quote from Jennie Allen's book. In it she says, "It's not easy to stop believing lies. We can't simply sit back and wait for our minds to heal, for our thoughts to change. We train. That's how truth gains the victory in the battle for our minds. We stick our heads in our Bibles day in and day out. ... We wake up in the morning, ... get on our knees and we submit our thoughts to Jesus. We invest in healthy relationships and intentionally go to them when we start to spiral. We choose well. Daily. Moment by moment. We train our minds." [55]

- In what ways might you start training your mind to look a little more like Philippians 4:8?

Philippians 4:10-13

WE CAN BE CONTENT IN ANY SITUATION THROUGH CHRIST'S STRENGTH.

To begin today, let's use our highlighter one last time.

- Highlight the word *"rejoiced"* in Philippians 4:10.

- Take a moment to flip back through the book of Philippians. Notice how many highlights you have for joy and rejoicing. What might you learn from this?

Philippians 4:10-13 starts out as a thank-you note. Something had prevented the Philippians from being able to send provisions to Paul. But when the window of opportunity finally opened, they jumped right in.

- Look at verse 18. What does this verse tell us about how they showed their concern to Paul?

- Are we actively looking for opportunities to help people? Do we jump at these opportunities when we see them? Why or why not?

Writing a thank-you note was a bit tricky for Paul. According to Bible scholar Dr. Steve Runge, "If he praises the gift too much, it will sound like he wants more. If he downplays it too much, he may sound ungrateful, or as if the gift was insufficient ..." [56] Paul wants to show his gratitude. But he also wants the church to know a very important principle.

- Complete Philippians 4:11.
  "Not that I am speaking of being in need, for ___ _____ _____ ___ _____ _____ ___ ___ ___ ___ _____."

The dictionary defines "content" as "being satisfied with what one is or has; not wanting more or anything else." [57]

- How has your "contentment" level been lately?

In Philippians 4:12, Paul says he knows contentment in:

- Being brought "_____" and when things "_____"

- *"In _____ and _____ circumstance"*

- When facing *"_____ and _____, _____ and _____."*

Look at the specific word used in verse 12:

- *"In any and every circumstance, I have learned the _____..."*

Let's look at what this secret isn't. The secret to contentment isn't based on circumstances. It isn't something in the future ... that illusive "something" that will finally make us satisfied. It isn't based at all on **what** we have.

- What IS the secret to contentment? (Write out Philippians 4:13)

Contentment is based on **Who** we have. C.S. Lewis said, "He who has God and everything else has no more than he who has God and nothing else." [58] We can face anything this life throws at us, but only in Christ's strength. And that, friend, is more than enough.

- What situation are you facing where you feel discontent? How can you look at it today from a position of Christ's strength?

Philippians 4:14-23

GENEROSITY IS A SACRIFICE PLEASING TO GOD.

Paul ends Philippians with one last "thank you" to the church for their generosity. Paul and the Christians at Philippi shared a close friendship. They were there for each other through all situations. Notice what Paul says in Philippians 4:15:

- *"in the beginning of the gospel, when I left _____..."* (This will be important in a moment.)

- *"... no church entered into partnership with me in giving and receiving..."* No church. Except who?

Let's turn over to 2 Corinthians 8:1-5. In Paul's letter to the church of Corinth, he mentions specifically the generosity of the *"churches of Macedonia."* Philippi specifically was in the region of Macedonia. We can make the connection that this paragraph in 2 Corinthians, then, is about the Philippians.

- What do we learn about the Philippians from 2 Corinthians 8:1-5?

- What do we learn about generosity from this passage?

Paul was not just glad about their giving for himself. As we discussed yesterday, Paul had learned to be content no matter what he had (or didn't have). Instead, he was glad to see the "*fruit*" that was increasing in them from the giving.

- How might generosity not only bless the receiver, but the giver as well?

- Has this ever been true in your own life?

In Philippians 4:18, the gift that the Philippians offered was referred to as "*a fragrant offering, a sacrifice acceptable and pleasing to God.*" Giving is a sacrifice. Not just of our money, but our time, talent, energy, thought, resources or even our pride and selfishness.

- Which of these is easiest for you to give? Which do you have a hard time giving?

A key component to this is found in the last two words of verse 18.

- "*... the gifts you sent, a fragrant offering, a sacrifice acceptable and pleasing ___ _____.*"

- What did Jesus say about what we do for others in Matthew 25:40?

Ultimately, our giving is for God. And because we are content in Christ, we can give generously. We can know and trust and believe and rest upon the statement of Philippians 4:19.

- We can be generous because we can trust what?

Paul ends his letter to his dear friends and fellow Christ-followers in Philippi with a final benediction. He sends his greetings as well as those of his companions. And he acknowledges, just as we do today, that all the words we have read, all the things we have learned, every stirring of the Holy Spirit in our lives as we have gone through this study, all of it is for one purpose alone.

- Copy the words of Philippians 4:20 below:

Weekend Reflections

This week, we covered joy, anxiety, our thought life, our level of contentment and reasons for generosity. But there is one particular line that sticks out for this weekend. We see it in Philippians 4:9, which says, *"What you have learned and received and heard and seen in me – **practice these things ...**"* (emphasis added).

This weekend, let's apply this to friendship. Pick one of the following areas to practice.

- Find a way to involve your friends in an activity that inspires rejoicing in the Lord.

- Is there a relationship that is making you feel anxious? Every time you feel an anxious thought coming on, stop to pray.

- How have your thoughts toward your relationships and friends been lately? Have any negative thoughts tried creeping in? This weekend, take another look at Philippians 4:8 and write statements about your friends that are true, honorable, lovely, etc. Then take a moment to thank God for the people in your life.

- Check in on your friends on a deeper level. Are they worried, anxious, feeling discontent? Listen to and encourage them this weekend.

- Team up with a friend and together find one way to be generous this weekend.

Let's not stop at simply learning the words of the Bible. Let's **practice** them together. Let's put them to work and watch God's Word come alive.

Prayer

Father, what a study this has been. We have learned so much about joy and friendship. Help us to now put it into practice. Move the words from our heads to our hearts. Help them take root, water them, grow them and produce fruit in us, Holy Spirit. We love You, and we thank You that You are everything we need. In Jesus' name, amen.

Reflect on Philippians

As we close out the book of Philippians, there are four main ideas I pray we take to heart.

FRIENDSHIP.

We need people. We were created for community and unity. We search out good examples to follow. We deal with disagreements and pursue relationships with others. We thank God for the gift of good friends.

JOY.

Joy despite our circumstances. In prison. Facing death. In hunger or surrounded by excess. Our joy is in Christ. He doesn't change. Therefore, neither does our source of joy. We really and truly can "rejoice always."

LIVE A LIFE THAT LOOKS LIKE JESUS.

He suffered. Christ humbled Himself, even to death. But He also rose to new life! He also has victory. This is the prize that awaits us as well. We can follow in His footsteps.

KNOW THAT JESUS IS EVERYTHING.

Life = Christ. Death = Gain. We cannot lose. The world cannot define us. We are His. Whatever we face, we can have peace. We can be content. We can give abundantly, because Jesus Christ is all we need.

Notes

Notes

_____

_____

_____

_____

_____

_____

_____

_____

_____

_____

_____

_____

_____

_____

_____

_____

_____

_____

_____

_____

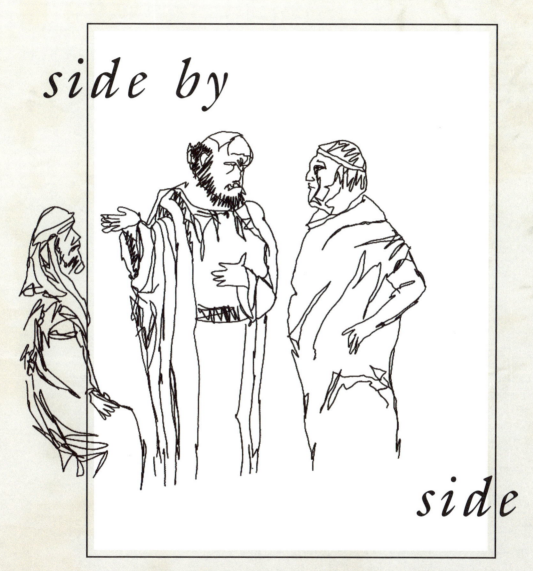

side by

side

"STANDING FIRM IN ONE SPIRIT, WITH ONE MIND STRIVING
SIDE BY SIDE FOR THE FAITH OF THE GOSPEL."

PHILIPPIANS 1:27

Jesus' Relationship With Women

BY WENDY BLIGHT

Though the culture surrounding the early church minimized the dignity of women, Jesus boldly affirmed women's worth and benefited greatly from their ministry.

JESUS SPOKE FREELY TO WOMEN, ESPECIALLY IN PUBLIC, AT A TIME WHEN MOST MEN DID NOT.

He ministered to the Samaritan woman at the well (John 4) as well as the woman caught in adultery. (John 8) Jesus addressed their situations and spoke gentle, sometimes hard, truth. More importantly, He extended grace and healed and restored their broken and hurting souls.

JESUS FREQUENTLY STOPPED WHAT HE WAS DOING AND/OR SAYING TO MINISTER TO HURTING WOMEN.

In **Luke 7**, as Jesus walked into the town of Nain, His eyes led Him to a grieving widow, standing in the midst of a crowd, who had just lost her only son. Jesus had compassion on her, comforting her, *"Don't cry"* (Luke 7:13, NIV). He then raised her son from the dead and gave him back to her.

In **Mark 1**, Jesus, after teaching in the synagogue, went to the home of Peter and Andrew. Peter told Jesus his mother-in-law was sick with a high fever. Jesus immediately healed her, and she got up and served them.

In **Matthew 9**, while Jesus was on His way to heal a Jewish leader's daughter, He encountered a woman who had been bleeding for 12 years. Matthew tells us she came up behind Jesus and touched the edge of his cloak, saying to herself, *"If I only touch his cloak, I will be healed."* Scripture tells us Jesus turned, saw her and spoke these words, *"'Take heart, daughter,' he said, 'your faith has healed you.' And the woman was healed at that moment."*

JESUS PRAISED WOMEN FOR THEIR FAITH.

In **Matthew 15**, Jesus healed the child of a Canaanite woman, a non-Jew. Why was this so significant? Jesus very rarely interacted with people who were not Jewish. God sent Him for the Jews. Yet, because of this woman's incredible faith to approach Him and boldly ask for her child's healing, He stepped outside of His assignment to honor and point out her great faith.

In **Mark 12**, Jesus praised a poor widow for her generosity. He pointed out to His disciples that by giving out of her poverty, she gave much more than the wealthy who gave out of their abundance.

JESUS ALLOWED WOMEN TO FOLLOW HIM AND MINISTER TO HIM!

Throughout Scripture, we see Jesus interacting with women in many other ways. Women anointed Jesus (Matthew 2; Luke 7). Women like Mary Magdalene, Joanna and Susanna helped Jesus financially (Luke 8) and still others, like Mary and Martha, offered Jesus the gift of hospitality. (Luke 10; John 12)

JESUS CHOSE WOMEN TO BE THE FIRST TO DISCOVER HIS EMPTY TOMB TO KNOW HE HAD TRULY RISEN FROM THE GRAVE.

Jesus chose women to discover, go and share the good news of His resurrection. (Matthew 28)

JESUS ALSO USED WOMEN AS ILLUSTRATIONS IN MANY OF HIS STORIES AND PARABLES.

The parable of the unjust judge and the widow. (Luke 18:1-8) The parable of the lost coin. (Luke 15:8-10) Jesus' favorable treatment of women carried forward into the early church in the lives and stories of Euodia and Syntyche (Philippians 4:2-3) and Lydia. Lydia is believed to be the first Christian convert in Macedonia who likely hosted and led the first house church in Philippi. (Acts 16:13-15, 40)

The very fact Jesus singled out women and treated them with kindness, compassion and dignity ... that He allowed them to support and minister to Him ... reveals that Jesus respected women and valued them greatly. He engaged with them and allowed them to use their giftedness to help Him in His Kingdom work!

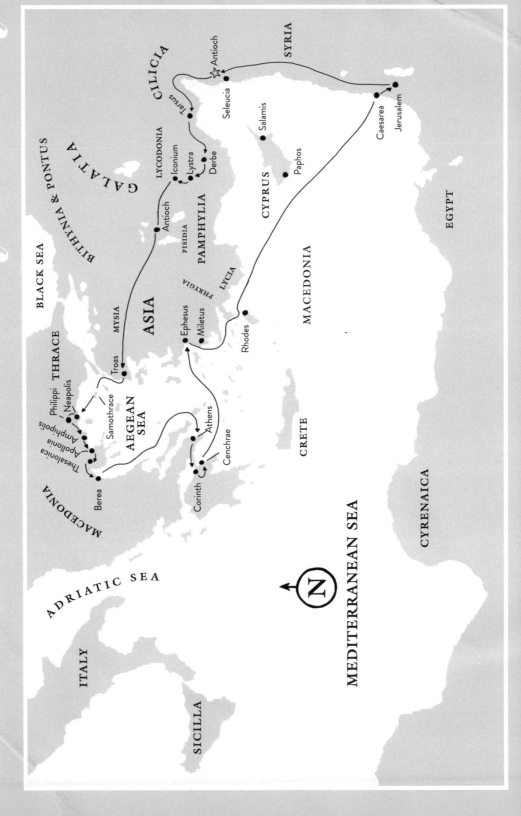

Paul's 2nd Missionary Journey

Epaphroditus with Paul and the Philippian Church

BY JOEL MUDDAMALLE

We live in a culture where the word "friend" is often used flippantly. We may introduce the person we just met to a group as "my friend." We may have acquaintances we refer to as friends. It may surprise us to see who is on our list of friends on social media. But who is a friend? How should friends act toward each other? And what is required to attain that coveted status as a trusted friend?

In Philippians, we are introduced to Epaphroditus. Epaphroditus was a common name in the Graeco-Roman world, and it meant "charming" or "handsome." Epaphroditus was a leader in the Philippian church and also a close friend of the Apostle Paul. It was Epaphroditus who was trusted to carry and deliver a financial gift from the Philippians to Paul, who was imprisoned. Unlike our modern prison systems, the ancient world did not provide many needs for prisoners. Therefore, this financial support during imprisonment was a *"fragrant offering"* and *"an acceptable sacrifice"* (Philippians 4:18) for Paul.

As we learn more about Epaphroditus, we find someone who is a dearly loved friend. Paul refers to him as his "brother," *"fellow worker"* and *"fellow soldier"* (Philippians 2:25). Just like many of our friendships, the relationship between Paul and Epaphroditus crossed into various categories of life. Epaphroditus had a close family and sibling relationship with Paul. In other words, there is a sense of intimacy. They are also working together toward the same goal. Their friendship is intimately connected to their work. Finally, the context of their work included a sense of danger that required a fierce loyalty to each other as is commonly found among soldiers. All of these dimensions and the nearness between Epaphroditus and Paul caused Paul to say they were spared *"sorrow upon sorrow"* (Philippians 2:27) when it seemed like Epaphroditus could have died from illness.

Clearly, Epaphroditus was the kind of friend that stood side by side with the mind of Christ, (Philippians 2:5-11) striving for the faith of the gospel with both his friends in the Philippian church and his friend Paul. Epaphroditus sacrificed and thought of the needs of others even at a cost to himself. This was the kind of friend Epaphroditus was and why Paul urged the Philippians to receive him back with joy and to show him honor. (Philippians 2:29)

This begs us to consider what kind of friend we are. In a culture and society that tempts us to be satisfied with acquaintances and surface-level friendships, Christ calls those within the church to a type of friendship that is rooted in sibling love, and that results in working toward the faithful proclamation of the good news of the gospel as soldiers of Christ. You and I have an opportunity to be to others, what Epaphroditus was to Paul and the Philippian church. So today, let's make the decision to pursue friendships that model the closeness of siblings who are fellow workers and soldiers for the sake of Christ.

Paul and Timothy

BY ERIC GAGNON

Timothy's name means "honoring to God" or "dear to God," and he was certainly a dear and honored friend to the Apostle Paul and others. His importance is underscored by the fact that two books of the Bible (1 and 2 Timothy) are addressed specifically to him. Timothy's name appears in 10 of the Pauline Epistles, six of which he is listed as a co-sender (1 Thessalonians 1:1; 2 Corinthians 1:1; Philippians 1:1; Philemon 1; 2 Thessalonians 1:1; Colossians 1:1).

Paul's beloved friend Timothy was regarded by him with tender affection. He is identified as we learned Epaphroditus was:

- *"our brother"* (1 Thessalonians 3:2; 2 Corinthians 1:1; Philemon 1)
- *"fellow worker"* (1 Thessalonians 3:2; Romans 16:21)

But Timothy was also identified as Paul's:

- *"beloved and faithful child in the Lord"* (1 Corinthians 4:17; 1 Timothy 1:2)
- *"true child in the faith"* (1 Timothy 1:2)

Perhaps the greatest record of friendship we have between Timothy and Paul is here in Philippians. Observe the care in the Apostle Paul's words about Timothy: "For I have no one like him, who will be genuinely concerned for your welfare. For they all seek their own interests, not those of Jesus Christ. But you know Timothy's proven worth, how as a son with a father he has served with me in the gospel" (Philippians 2:20-22).

Timothy assisted Paul throughout his missionary journeys and imprisonments, even likely becoming imprisoned himself. (Hebrews 13:23) According to later tradition preserved by Eusebius, Timothy, the disciple of Paul, became the first bishop of Ephesus.

As Christians, we often experience a bond with fellow believers that is closer than biological family members. Paul and Timothy model for us the friendship that can be had in Christ between a disciple and his teacher, a father and his child. God in Christ (John 1:1,14) also models this for us when he says, "No longer do I call you servants, for the servant does not know what his master is doing; but I have called you friends" (John 15:15).

When Friends Disagree

BY KAYLA FERRIS

Through Philippians, we see the rich friendship between Paul and the church of Philippi. However, Paul was no stranger to friendship challenges. Case in point: Paul's early ministry partner and friend, Barnabas.

The name Barnabas literally means "son of encouragement" (Acts 4:36), a perfect description for this man. When the apostles of Jerusalem would not accept Paul as a new convert, it was Barnabas who stood up and befriended Paul. (Acts 9:26-27) Together, Barnabas and Paul shared the gospel during their first missionary journey.

However, before Paul's second missionary journey, an issue arose between the friends. Acts 15:36-41 tells us that they had a "sharp disagreement." Barnabas wanted to take along a man named John Mark. Paul did not. The text goes on to say "so ... they separated from each other." What exactly happened between these friends and what can we learn from it?

1. SOMETIMES WE CAN DISAGREE AND BOTH BE RIGHT.

During their first journey, John Mark had deserted them along the way. Barnabas was arguing to give John Mark a second chance. However, Paul just couldn't allow for the gospel to be weakened by someone who wasn't all in. As pastor Bob Deffinbaugh describes in his book, When Division Becomes Multiplication, both men were acting in accordance to their spiritual gifting. Barnabas' gifts were mercy and encouragement. He wouldn't give up on John Mark, similar to the way he had stood up for Paul long ago. Paul's gifts were leadership and passion for the gospel. He was ready to suffer for the sake of Christ, and he needed leaders who would do the same. Neither one was wrong.

2. SOMETIMES DISAGREEMENTS CAN PROVE TO BE BENEFICIAL.

Both men stood unwavering in their convictions, and when they reached an impasse, they agreed to respectfully disagree. Several amazing things took place because of this. For example, their disagreement took them in different directions, resulting in even more people receiving the gospel message. Also, look at the new people who entered their close circles and how those lives changed. John Mark was given that second chance, and it changed his life. Together, John Mark and Barnabas made a huge impact on the early church. Without Barnabas by his side, Paul then invited Silas and Timothy into his ministry. These men benefited from Paul's passion and teaching and went on to make a huge impact as well. This division, in the hands of God, turned into multiplication.

3. RECONCILIATION IS POSSIBLE IN JESUS.

Many years later, in 1 Corinthians 9:6, Paul speaks of himself and Barnabas as friends and partners in ministry. And in 2 Timothy 4:11, Paul even asks Timothy to return with John Mark, because in Paul's own words, "he is very useful to me for ministry." These friends may have taken different paths, but their friendship was reconciled under the common cause of Christ.

When it comes to our friendships, maybe it's okay to respectfully agree to disagree. Perhaps your friend is approaching the situation with a different spiritual gift than you. And yes, sometimes separation happens. But in those moments, remember that what looks like a painful division might be the very thing God uses to bring multiplication. And finally, don't give up on friendship. Don't check out when it gets hard. Stick with it and see what God can do.

Identifying the Hurdles of Friendship: _____

PHILIPPIANS 1:9-11

"And it is my prayer that your love may abound more and more, with knowledge and all discernment, so that you may approve what is excellent, and so be pure and blameless for the day of Christ, filled with the fruit of righteousness that comes through Jesus Christ, to the glory and praise of God."

CATEGORY: CRITICISM

It's much easier to try to change someone else through criticism rather than ask God in prayer what we first need to address within ourselves. Someone with a critical spirit points fingers at others instead of looking inward at what they may need to work on and grow in.

Key: Seek a loving understanding through Jesus that goes beyond our own thoughts and opinions.

In a conflict or misunderstanding with another person, it is so easy to become utterly convinced that our vantage point is the only vantage point. I do this; we all do this. And yet, the more we focus on what the other person is always doing wrong, the less we will recognize what they are doing right. Research has shown that for every negative or critical interaction, it will take five positive interactions to counterbalance that. [1]

When we criticize another person, studies also show that it can cause that person to become less and less responsive to any kind of emotion. Children with a highly critical parent often stop paying attention to facial expressions of any kind and are much more prone to anxiety and depression.[2]

So, what does all of this research have to do with what Paul wrote in Philippians 1? Paul is presenting a future hope through the phrase *"for the day of Christ"* as seen in Philippians 1:10. Later, he uses a similar idea in Philippians 4:5 when he says *"the Lord is at hand."* Paul has these end times implications woven all through Philippians. He uses a variety of phrases such as *"day of the Lord,"* or *"the day is near"* or *"at hand."* The day of the Lord perspective is key to understanding and being motivated to walk through our present circumstances.

This deeper motivation should remind us of how important our actions and reactions are toward one another. In the prayer in Philippians 1, Paul says our love should abound more and more with knowledge and depth of insight so that we can discern what is best. Though he isn't specifically referencing "criticism" here, he is encouraging us to use godly wisdom and discernment so we can stay pure and blameless in all our words and actions.

[1] https://collectivehub.com/2017/05/how-many-good-experiences-finally-outweigh-a-bad-one/
[2] https://www.sciencedaily.com/releases/2018/06/180611133507.htm

As Christ-followers, we should display evidence of the work of Christ in us — the fruit of righteousness (Philippians 1:11) — and exchange our critical responses for loving responses. If the seeds we plant in our friendships are full of criticism, the fruit of those friendships will be disunity. If our seeds are full of prayer and mature love, the fruit will be unity.

Now What: In Philippians 1:15, Paul reminds us that part of laying down our criticism is remembering to be less concerned about others' motives, and more concerned about keeping Christ preached front and center. In other words, let's always try to keep the main thing the main thing. As Paul wraps up the chapter in Philippians 1:27, we are reminded we can't control the conduct of others, but we can control our conduct. The greatest message we will ever preach to this world is not simply with our words, but with how we treat others and live our lives.

PHILIPPIANS 4:8-9

"Finally, brothers, whatever is true, whatever is honorable, whatever is just, whatever is pure, whatever is lovely, whatever is commendable, if there is any excellence, if there is anything worthy of praise, think about these things. What you have learned and received and heard and seen in me—practice these things, and the God of peace will be with you."

CATEGORY: BITTERNESS

Lacking trust in God to address the hurt others have caused you, harboring resentments and unforgiveness.

Imagine for a moment that God's Word here was stated in the negative sense. It might read something like, "Finally, brothers, whatever is false, whatever is dishonorable, whatever is criminal, whatever is filthy, whatever is hideous, whatever is shameful, if there is any mediocrity, if there is anything worthy of harsh rebuke, don't become **bitter** by setting your mind on these things." Instead, God saw fit to state what it is we should be thinking about, and I'm grateful for that. However, considering these negatives can help us understand the positives.

These verses here in Philippians 4:8-9 immediately follow the Apostle Paul's direct address to two specific women to *"agree in the Lord"* (Philippians 4:2). It's amazing that Paul, knowing this letter would be read by multiple people, still chose to address these two women specifically by name, "Euodia" and "Syntyche." It was a personal address. In the same verse, Paul said he was entreating these women to agree. The word translated "entreat" in the ESV was originally written *parakaleō* in Greek. It is a great translation because it means to ask someone strongly or earnestly. The NIV also gets at this meaning well with the word *plead: "I plead with Euodia and I plead with Syntyche to be of the same mind in the Lord."* Other root forms of this word parakaleō in Scripture includes "encouragement" (Acts 4:36) and *"exhortation"* (Hebrews 13:22), and even refers to our Helper, the Holy Spirit. (John 14:26) So, this personal address to Euodia and Syntyche is more than a simple ask to get along, whatever their quarrel was.

Key: When it comes to unity within the body of Christ and friendship with one another, we can learn from this pleading from God's Word that it is very important for us all to *"agree in the Lord."*

While we might not always know how to do this, God did not leave us without the answer. In Philippians 4:8-9, the verses that follow Pauls's address, we discover the connection. The reason we can *"agree in the Lord"* is not because we agree with every single thought another person has. More often, what happens in our relationships is that we get frustrated or hurt in some way. And instead of setting our minds on things above, we dwell in bitterness on all the negatives.

Now what: Instead, we should be encouraged that despite whatever differences we have with other believers, we can hold on tightly together to what we have in common: the Lord. This is what is true, honorable, just, pure, lovely, commendable, excellent and worthy of praise. These are descriptions of Christ, and dwelling on Him through our relationships is how we can be sure *"the God of peace will be with you"* (Philippians 4:9).

PHILIPPIANS 2:3-4, ESV

"Do nothing from selfish ambition or conceit, but in humility count others more significant than yourselves. Let each of you look not only to his own interests, but also to the interests of others."

CATEGORY: PRIDE

We all want to be right. But at what cost? When taken to the extreme, the desire to be right can often mean sacrificing humility and creating greater animosity in a relationship. When we refuse to do our part, get immediately defensive in order to prove our point, and constantly interrupt the other person to discredit what they are saying, the result will be conflict escalation rather than resolution. Lysa TerKeurst challenges herself in these situations with a very arresting question, "Would I rather prove that I'm right or improve this relationship? I can't do both at the same time." Pride is very costly.

Key: We often think of humility as a position of weakness. In reality, it's the only posture that infuses us with the strength and wisdom of Jesus. And remember, humility isn't you presenting yourself as less than ... it's the only way to shift the atmosphere from hard to hopeful.

Paul teaches us the importance of humility by ultimately pointing to Christ. We understand the meaning of Philippians 2:1-5 when we see humility in action through Christ's willingness to experience humanity and when we learn obedience through His suffering. (Philippians 2:6-11) The humility of Christ was purposeful. Christ, through His humility, made it possible for us to be healed. The journey of humility for Christ took Him to the cross but ended in His exaltation, *"so that at the name of Jesus every knee should bow, in heaven and on earth and under the earth, and every tongue confess that Jesus Christ is Lord, to the glory of God the Father"* (Philippians 2:10).

Exercising humility in our friendships doesn't come easily or naturally. However, it is necessary. When we embrace humility, we embrace Christ. We participate in the life of Christ. The more we exercise humility, the greater we will learn obedience to God. And friends, one of the greatest testing grounds for humility is in our friendships.

Remember, humility isn't letting people walk over you or take advantage of you, seeing yourself as less than or not worthy to be loved and respected. But it is willingly choosing to look more and more like Christ, especially in the harder, potentially holy, moments of relationships.

Now What: We have two options when it comes to how we view humility. We can view it through the lens of man or the lens of God. When we view humility through the lens of man, we think less of ourselves, resulting in feelings of shame and doubt. Ultimately, this lens is destructive to ourselves and our friendships. However, when we view ourselves through the lens of God, we don't think less of ourselves, we think of God more. We see ourselves with the eyes of God, and this is the best way to see.

To conclude, meditate and reflect on Paul's words in Philippians 2:13-16.

"...for it is God who works in you, both to will and to work for his good pleasure. Do all things without grumbling or disputing, that you may be blameless and innocent, children of God without blemish in the midst of a crooked and twisted generation, among whom you shine as lights in the world, holding fast to the word of life, so that in the day of Christ I may be proud that I did not run in vain or labor in vain."

PHILIPPIANS 3:7-8
"But whatever gain I had, I counted as loss for the sake of Christ. Indeed, I count everything as loss because of the surpassing worth of knowing Christ Jesus my Lord. For his sake I have suffered the loss of all things and count them as rubbish, in order that I may gain Christ."

CATEGORY: SUPERIORITY

In businesses or sporting arenas, competition seems to push people to achieve their best. However, the entire premise behind competition is the idea that someone will come out on top, proving themselves to be "better than" another. While some will argue this is a good model for business, I think we can universally agree this is a bad model for friendship. A spirit of superiority is like one person sucking all of the oxygen out of the relationship. The fire eventually goes out.

Key: Comparing oneself to one's friends will lead to feelings of superiority or inferiority. Instead, as followers of Christ, our worth and value are found in Jesus. And in Jesus, we are all on equal ground.

The Philippian Christians faced a struggle. There were Jewish Christians among them who began to teach that to be Christian, you first needed to become a Jew. Those who were Jewish prided themselves on their circumcision and special place in history as God's people. As a result, they looked down on gentile Christians. A spirit of superiority began to grow.

Paul tells his friends in Philippi that if anyone had any right to brag in Jewish superiority, it was him. He had all the right qualifications, and yet Paul called his high qualifications *"rubbish."* Paul said his only worth and value came from *"knowing Christ Jesus my Lord"* (Philippians 3:8).

When we compare ourselves to our friends, often one of two things can occur. We might develop feelings of superiority. We start to believe an exaggerated view of our own importance, and expect others to believe it as well. It is nearly impossible to properly love someone when we are looking down on them and forcing them to look up at us. Or, comparing might cause us to develop feelings of inferiority. We start to feel like maybe we are "less than" others. This can lead to a number of struggles, including resentment, depression or even idolatry.

Now What: The best way to walk in healthy friendships is to know your worth and value in Jesus Christ. In Jesus, we are all sinners, saved only by His grace. He alone is superior. Yet also in Jesus, we are all loved, cherished and valued. Jesus not only loves you; He also likes you. When we know our worth in Jesus, we are free to walk away from comparison and competition, and instead, walk with our friends in truth and love.

"... complete my joy by being of the same mind, having the same love, being in full accord and of one mind. Do nothing from selfish ambition or conceit, but in humility count others more significant than yourselves. Let each of you look not only to his own interests, but also to the interests of others."
Philippians 2:2-4

In Case You Were Wondering

SOMETIMES THERE IS MORE TO UNDERSTANDING SCRIPTURE THAN ORIGINALLY MEETS THE EYE. THAT'S WHY OUR TEAM WANTED TO PROVIDE YOU WITH ADDITIONAL INFORMATION ON SOME OF THE MOST POPULAR VERSES FROM PHILIPPIANS.

1. "AND I AM SURE OF THIS, THAT HE WHO BEGAN A GOOD WORK IN YOU WILL BRING IT TO COMPLETION AT THE DAY OF JESUS CHRIST" (PHILIPPIANS 1:6).

We can be quick to apply a verse like Philippians 1:6 individually to "me" and "my own life." And certainly it can be applied that way. We can be sure God finishes what He starts. However, the good work the Apostle Paul is so confident about in the Philippians is their *koinonia* or "partnership" in the gospel, which Paul mentions at least six times in the short letter to the Philippians. The Philippian church's partnership in the proclamation of the gospel was a work God started, and they could be sure that He intended to finish it until Jesus' return. Let it be said that we have the book of Philippians today, speaking the gospel to us, because of this partnership! It is remarkable that there is nothing apparently controversial when Paul states that the actions of the Philippians are the work of God. That those two things are not at odds with each other is clear in the way it rolls off of Paul's tongue. Being humbled that our works are the working of God in His Church, we can be confident in God — not only that He finishes what He starts in us individually, but that He is building His Church in the same way. (Matthew 16:18)

2. "FOR TO ME TO LIVE IS CHRIST, AND TO DIE IS GAIN" (PHILIPPIANS 1:21).

We know Paul suffered much, and some have proposed that in Philippians 1:21 Paul was expressing the Greek philosophy of the culture around him which proclaimed that death was a welcome escape from the suffering of this life. However, The Bible does not speak about death as a welcome end to suffering. And this isn't what Paul was saying either. In fact, he tells us in the next couple of verses exactly why, to him, death is gain. *"My desire is to depart and be with Christ, for that is far better"* (Philippians 1:23). Death is not gain if we arrive there and do not have Jesus. In 1 Corinthians 15:19, Paul states that if our hope is in vain, we as Christians are of all people on earth the most to be pitied. This is because, if we truly live as Christians, life will actually be much harder in many ways. But since we have a sure and certain hope in Christ, we are joyful in this life, even amidst suffering, and we are even more eager for the next.

3. "ONLY LET YOUR MANNER OF LIFE BE WORTHY OF THE GOSPEL OF CHRIST, SO THAT WHETHER I COME AND SEE YOU OR AM ABSENT, I MAY HEAR OF YOU THAT YOU ARE STANDING FIRM IN ONE SPIRIT, WITH ONE MIND STRIVING SIDE BY SIDE FOR THE FAITH OF THE GOSPEL" (PHILIPPIANS 1:27).

It is clear that Philippians 1:27 is about Christian unity. Despite their differences, we can see Paul strongly encourage the Philippian church to be of *"one mind"* and to work *"side by side."* Some have taken this to mean that there should never be disagreements among Christians, or that divisions and denominations are wrong. Yet, we know in his letter to the Corinthians regarding their unity around the Lord's Supper, Paul stated, *"there must be factions among you in order that those who are genuine among you may be recognized"* (1 Corinthians 11:19). So it must be possible to work side by side, without always agreeing with each other about every detail. The key for how to do this is found at the end of the verse. Side by side for what? *"for the faith of the gospel."*

Our unity as the one Church under Christ is around the message of the gospel of God: that a perfect and holy God made the world good, that mankind has all sinned and gone astray, that God the Son took on human flesh, lived a perfect life, died on the cross as the payment for our sin and rose to life in order that all who place their trust in Him, would be saved from all sin, death and God's holy wrath and judgment. This gives us a lot to be unified about. And this is the undeniably clear message from our Lord in which all Christians everywhere can find their unity in proclaiming throughout the world.

4. "DO NOTHING FROM SELFISH AMBITION OR CONCEIT, BUT IN HUMILITY COUNT OTHERS MORE SIGNIFICANT THAN YOURSELVES" (PHILIPPIANS 2:3).

In a world that promotes taking pride in everything we do, this verse can feel like a shock of lightning. Philippians 2:3 tells us that not only only should we do away with self-focused ambition, but that we should also count all others *"more significant!"* In the Greek culture of Philippi, hubris was praised and humility was ridiculed. It was therefore very countercultural to be told to be like Christ who humbled himself. (Philippians 2:8) The Apostle Paul was not telling believers to think less of themselves, but as he states elsewhere, not too highly. (Romans 12:3) In addition, the word used here for "more significant" is used later on in respect to the *"surpassing"* worth of knowing Christ Jesus. (Philippians 3:8) Knowing Jesus far surpasses the importance of everything else, but that doesn't mean everything else is worthless. The same word describes the peace of God, which *transcends* all understanding. (Philippians 4:7) The peace of God *surpasses* the comprehension of all human understanding, but it doesn't make all other understanding worthless. If we all considered each other more significant than ourselves, we would be so lifted up by others that selfish ambitions would be the furthest thing from our thoughts.

5. "... THOUGH HE WAS IN THE FORM OF GOD, DID NOT COUNT EQUALITY WITH GOD A THING TO BE GRASPED BUT EMPTIED HIMSELF, BY TAKING THE FORM OF A SERVANT, BEING BORN IN THE LIKENESS OF MEN" (PHILIPPIANS 2:6-7).

This Scripture concisely affirms both the divinity and the humanity of Jesus. It has been used to wrongly emphasize one or the other. Either the focus is given to Jesus having only the "form" of God, meaning He is merely human, or the focus is given to Jesus only having the "likeness" of men, making Him not really human. Yet a careful study of these words reveals the incredible miracle that Scripture teaches about Jesus: He is fully God and fully man. What does it mean that Jesus has the *likeness* of men except that He is God? And what is the point of pointing out the form of God except that He is human? Possibly the clearest other example in Scripture is 2 Corinthians 4:4-6, where the Apostle Paul writes about the *"the **glory** of Christ, who is the **image** of God ... For God, who said, 'Let light shine out of darkness,' has shone in our hearts to give the light of the knowledge of the **glory** of God in the **face** of Jesus Christ"* (2 Corinthians 4:4-6, emphasis added). The glory of God in the Old Testament is always associated with tangible manifestations of the invisible God. So these verses link Christ with the image of God, in which *humanity* is made, and with the *glory* of God, which only God possesses.

6. "DO ALL THINGS WITHOUT GRUMBLING OR DISPUTING" (PHILIPPIANS 2:14).

When the Apostle Paul penned Philippians 2:14, he had in mind the grumbling and complaining of the Israelites against God in the desert, which he specifically mentions in 1 Corinthians 10. "Grumbling" in the original Greek carries a connotation of private complaining. And "disputing" usually refers to evil thinking, unholy reasoning or doubts about God. Knowing all the Israelites endured in the desert, we might think they had reason to doubt or complain privately. Yet, their example shows us that God still desires integrity and faithfulness from His people even in experiencing *suffering and persecution* for being followers of Christ. (Philippians 1:29) It also seems likely, based on looking at the entire letter to the Philippians, that the Philippians were grumbling against their leaders in the church, much like the Israelites grumbled against Moses. The biggest lesson from this verse then is this: If the Philippians were not to complain even privately about their very real suffering and persecution, how much less should we grumble about the leaders in our churches and our own circumstances? This doesn't mean we withhold concerns or fail to hold our leaders accountable, but there is an overall attitude of love and trust that God's people should always have for one another, especially the ones He has put as watchmen over our souls. (Hebrews 13:17)

7. "INDEED, I COUNT EVERYTHING AS LOSS BECAUSE OF THE SURPASSING WORTH OF KNOWING CHRIST JESUS MY LORD. FOR HIS SAKE I HAVE SUFFERED THE LOSS OF ALL THINGS AND COUNT THEM AS RUBBISH, IN ORDER THAT I MAY GAIN CHRIST" (PHILIPPIANS 3:8).

When we truly encounter Jesus Christ and what He has done for us in making a way to God the Father, we, like Paul, should consider the very best of all of our thoughts, words and actions like garbage — as far as its usefulness for gaining right-standing with God and knowing Jesus as Lord. If we don't, we don't truly know Christ. On the other hand, there is no need to fall into the line of thinking that we can never do anything good. In the first part of this letter to the Philippians, the Apostle Paul encourages them to be *"filled with the fruit of righteousness that comes through Jesus Christ, to the glory and praise of God"* (Philippians 1:11). After we understand Jesus to have surpassing worth compared to everything else in the world, we are able to thank God with our lives, loving others and doing right. This is called "the fruit of righteousness," and it is a delight to God. It only becomes garbage if we think it counts for gaining salvation from sin, death or judgment — only Christ accomplishes that for us.

8. "DO NOT BE ANXIOUS ABOUT ANYTHING, BUT IN EVERYTHING BY PRAYER AND SUPPLICATION WITH THANKSGIVING LET YOUR REQUESTS BE MADE KNOWN TO GOD" (PHILIPPIANS 4:6).

For many of us, the command to not be anxious may be a hard one to follow. Even the most carefree among us tend to worry every now and then. Yet, in Philippians 4:6, we are not allowed the benefit of having even one anxiety. We are told not to be anxious about *anything*.

Jesus also told us not to be anxious. (Matthew 6:25) In our struggle against anxiety, we are not simply left with do's and don'ts, but with an alternative: prayer. And not just any prayer. The Greek word translated "requests" means specific things for which we are to ask God. Each time we have a specific concern or worry, we have just received something for which to pray specifically and deliberately. We don't need to sit in silence, trying to think of what to pray. Pray for every worry and concern! We do this with confidence, knowing that God must want to answer the prayers that are the very alternative to the anxiety He told us to avoid.

9. "I CAN DO ALL THINGS THROUGH HIM WHO STRENGTHENS ME" (PHILIPPIANS 4:13).

In Philippians 4:13, the Apostle Paul is not claiming omnipotence; he is explaining how the great contentment he described earlier is possible. One clue that this is the case is the Greek word *panta*, which means "all" not necessarily "things." The NIV translates it this way: *"I know what it is to be in need, and I know what it is to have plenty. I have learned the secret of being content in any and every situation, whether well fed or hungry, whether living in plenty or in want. I can do **all this** through him who gives me strength"* (emphasis added). So, instead of viewing this as a motto to achieve every goal we set out to accomplish, when we think of this verse we ought to think of the strength needed from Christ to accomplish an even greater miracle: contentment in all circumstances.

10. "AND MY GOD WILL SUPPLY EVERY NEED OF YOURS ACCORDING TO HIS RICHES IN GLORY IN CHRIST JESUS" (PHILIPPIANS 4:19).

In Philippians 4:19, the Apostle Paul is writing from prison and amazingly he says he is well supplied. Let us remember this when we think about what it means to have our needs met. It isn't saying, "God will make sure I'm comfortable in life," but that our needs will be supplied according to his riches *"in glory in Christ Jesus."* Elsewhere Paul specifies the nature of these riches of God as *"the riches of his kindness and forbearance and patience"* (Romans 2:4) and *"the riches and wisdom and knowledge of God"* (Romans 11:33). Similar verses which define these riches of God include Colossians 1:27; 2:2 and Ephesians 1:7–8; 3:8. Certainly we can trust God will take care of our physical needs. However, that clearly only seems to be part of the picture here in Paul's letter to the Philippians. Supplying our every need according to His riches in glory in Christ Jesus apparently includes a life being lived out in prison, and if that is God's will, we should want it. If meeting our needs was only physical, Paul couldn't have wanted suffering, which is at least part of what it means to know Christ: *"I want to know Christ—yes, to know the power of his resurrection and participation in his sufferings"* (Philippians 3:10, NIV).

End Notes

The History and Culture of Philippi
[1] Chapman, David. Philippians: Rejoicing and Thanksgiving. Focus on the Bible. Scotland, UK: Christian Focus Publications, 2012. pp. 12.

DAY 1
[2] Chapman, David. Philippians: Rejoicing and Thanksgiving. Focus on the Bible. Scotland, UK: Christian Focus Publications, 2012. pp. 37.

[3] Chapman, David. Philippians: Rejoicing and Thanksgiving. Focus on the Bible. Scotland, UK: Christian Focus Publications, 2012. pp. 38.

DAY 2
[4] Aristotle, Eth. Nic. 8.12.1.

DAY 3
[5] Chapman, David. Philippians: Rejoicing and Thanksgiving. Focus on the Bible. Scotland, UK: Christian Focus Publications, 2012. pp. 48.

[6] Henry, M. Matthew Henry's commentary on the whole Bible: complete and unabridged in one volume. Peabody: Hendrickson, 1994. pp. 2321.

[7] The ESV Study Bible. Wheaton, IL: Crossway, 2008. pp. 2280.

[8] Peterson, Eugene H. The Message Remix: The Bible in Contemporary Language. Colorado Springs, CO: Alive Communications, 2003. pp. 2134

[9] Peterson, Eugene H. The Message Remix: The Bible in Contemporary Language. Colorado Springs, CO: Alive Communications, 2003. pp. 2135

[10] Barry, J. D., Mangum, D., Brown, D. R., Heiser, M. S., Custis, M., Ritzema, E., ... Bomar, D. Faithlife Study Bible. Bellingham, WA: Lexham Press, 2012, 2016. (Php 1:9)

DAY 4
[11] Barry, J. D., Mangum, D., Brown, D. R., Heiser, M. S., Custis, M., Ritzema, E., ... Bomar, D. Faithlife Study Bible. Bellingham, WA: Lexham Press, 2012, 2016. (Php 1:12)

[12] Barclay, W. The Letters to Philippians, Colossians, and Thessalonians (3rd ed. fully rev. and updated, p. 26). Louisville, KY; London: Westminster John Knox Press, 2003. pp. 24.

DAY 5
[13] The ESV Study Bible. Wheaton, IL: Crossway, 2008. pp. 2281.

[14] Hansen, G. W. The Letter to the Philippians. Grand Rapids, MI; Nottingham, England: William B. Eerdmans Publishing Company, 2009. pp. 72.

[15] Barclay, W. The Letters to Philippians, Colossians, and Thessalonians (3rd ed. fully rev. and updated, p. 26). Louisville, KY; London: Westminster John Knox Press, 2003. pp. 28.

End Notes

DAY 6

[16] Hansen, G. W. The Letter to the Philippians. Grand Rapids, MI; Nottingham, England: William B. Eerdmans Publishing Company, 2009. pp. 77.

[17] Hamel, Dan. Philippians: The Joy of Christ. Autumn 2015. Southland Christian Church Small Group, Nicholasville, KY. pp. 20.

[18] Barclay, W. The Letters to Philippians, Colossians, and Thessalonians (3rd ed. fully rev. and updated, p. 26). Louisville, KY; London: Westminster John Knox Press, 2003. pp. 33.

DAY 7

[19] The ESV Study Bible. Wheaton, IL: Crossway, 2008. pp. 2282.

DAY 8

[20] Motyer, J.A. The Message of Philippians. The Bible Speaks Today, edited by John R. W. Stott. Downers Grove, IL: InterVarsity Press, 1984. pp. 98.

[21] Chapman, David. Philippians: Rejoicing and Thanksgiving. Focus on the Bible. Scotland, UK: Christian Focus Publications, 2012. pp. 91.

DAY 9

[22] Peterson, Eugene H. The Message Remix: The Bible in Contemporary Language. Colorado Springs, CO: Alive Communications, 2003. pp. 2136.

[23] Hansen, G. W. The Letter to the Philippians. Grand Rapids, MI; Nottingham, England: William B. Eerdmans Publishing Company, 2009. pp. 112.

[24] Martin, R. P. Philippians: An Introduction and Commentary. Downers Grove, IL: InterVarsity Press, 1987. pp. 101.

[25] Hamel, Dan. Philippians: The Joy of Christ. Autumn 2015. Southland Christian Church Small Group, Nicholasville, KY. pp. 25.

DAY 10

[26] Barclay, W. The Letters to Philippians, Colossians, and Thessalonians (3rd ed. fully rev. and updated, p. 26). Louisville, KY; London: Westminster John Knox Press, 2003. pp. 41.

[27] The ESV Study Bible. Wheaton, IL: Crossway, 2008. pp. 2283.

DAY 11

[28] Wilkins, Jen. "How Salvation Brings Freedom." The Gospel Coalition. www.thegospelcoalition.org/article/how-salvation-brings-freedom. Accessed August 2020.

[29] Wilkins, Jen. "How Salvation Brings Freedom." The Gospel Coalition. www.thegospelcoalition.org/article/how-salvation-brings-freedom. Accessed August 2020.

[30] Dictionary of Biblical Languages with Semantic Domains; Greek (New Testament)

End Notes

DAY 13

[31] Barclay, W. The Letters to Philippians, Colossians, and Thessalonians (3rd ed. fully rev. and updated, p. 26). Louisville, KY; London: Westminster John Knox Press, 2003. pp. 56.

[32] Henry, M. Matthew Henry's commentary on the whole Bible: complete and unabridged in one volume. Peabody: Hendrickson, 1994. pp. 2325.

DAY 14

[33] Barclay, W. The Letters to Philippians, Colossians, and Thessalonians (3rd ed. fully rev. and updated, p. 26). Louisville, KY; London: Westminster John Knox Press, 2003. pp. 57.

[34] Runge, S. E. "Why Paul Considered Epaphroditus Successful." In Faithlife Study Bible. Bellingham, WA: Lexham Press, 2012, 2016.

[35] Barclay, W. The Letters to Philippians, Colossians, and Thessalonians (3rd ed. fully rev. and updated, p. 26). Louisville, KY; London: Westminster John Knox Press, 2003. pp. 58-59.

[36] Barry, J. D., Mangum, D., Brown, D. R., Heiser, M. S., Custis, M., Ritzema, E., ... Bomar, D. Faithlife Study Bible. Bellingham, WA: Lexham Press, 2012, 2016. (Php 2:29)

DAY 15

[37] Hamel, Dan. Philippians: The Joy of Christ. Autumn 2015. Southland Christian Church Small Group, Nicholasville, KY. pp. 36.

[38] The ESV Study Bible. Wheaton, IL: Crossway, 2008. pp. 2285.

[39] Barclay, W. The Letters to Philippians, Colossians, and Thessalonians (3rd ed. fully rev. and updated, p. 26). Louisville, KY; London: Westminster John Knox Press, 2003. pp. 64.

DAY 17

[40] Hamel, Dan. Philippians: The Joy of Christ. Autumn 2015. Southland Christian Church Small Group, Nicholasville, KY. pp. 39.

DAY 18

[41] The ESV Study Bible. Wheaton, IL: Crossway, 2008. pp. 2286.

[42] Barclay, W. The Letters to Philippians, Colossians, and Thessalonians (3rd ed. fully rev. and updated, p. 26). Louisville, KY; London: Westminster John Knox Press, 2003. pp. 78.

[43] Henry, M. Matthew Henry's commentary on the whole Bible: complete and unabridged in one volume. Peabody: Hendrickson, 1994. pp. 2327.

DAY 19

[44] Hamel, Dan. Philippians: The Joy of Christ. Autumn 2015. Southland Christian Church Small Group, Nicholasville, KY. pp. 46.

[45] The ESV Study Bible. Wheaton, IL: Crossway, 2008. pp. 2286.

End Notes

DAY 20

[46] Barclay, W. The Letters to Philippians, Colossians, and Thessalonians (3rd ed. fully rev. and updated, p. 26). Louisville, KY; London: Westminster John Knox Press, 2003. pp. 87.

DAY 21

[47] Barclay, W. The Letters to Philippians, Colossians, and Thessalonians (3rd ed. fully rev. and updated, p. 26). Louisville, KY; London: Westminster John Knox Press, 2003. pp. 88.

[48] Peterson, Eugene H. The Message Remix: The Bible in Contemporary Language. Colorado Springs, CO: Alive Communications, 2003. pp. 2139.

[49] The ESV Study Bible. Wheaton, IL: Crossway, 2008. pp. 2287.

DAY 22

[50] Hamel, Dan. Philippians: The Joy of Christ. Autumn 2015. Southland Christian Church Small Group, Nicholasville, KY. pp. 54.

[51] Bengel, Johann A. Gnomon of the New Testament. StudyLight.org, 2001-2020. www.studylight.org/commentaries/jab/philippians-4.html. Accessed August 2020.

[52] "A Quote by Ralph Waldo Emerson." Good Reads, www.goodreads.com/quotes/14132-cultivate-the-habit-of-being-grateful-for-every-good-thing. Accessed August 2020.

DAY 23

[53] Allen, Jennie. Get Out of Your Head. Colorado Springs, CO: WaterBrook, 2020. pp. 10.

[54] Allen, Jennie. Get Out of Your Head. Colorado Springs, CO: WaterBrook, 2020. pp. 42-43.

[55] Allen, Jennie. Get Out of Your Head. Colorado Springs, CO: WaterBrook, 2020. pp. 212-213.

DAY 24

[56] Runge, S. E. High Definition Commentary: Philippians. Bellingham, WA: Lexham Press, 2011. (Php 4:10–20).

[57] "Content." Dictionary.com, LLC., 2020. www.dictionary.com/browse/content. Accessed August 2020.

[58] Lewis, C.S. "The Weight of Glory." Good Reads, www.goodreads.com/quotes/81966-he-who-has-god-and-everything-else-has-no-more. Accessed August 2020.

About Proverbs 31 Ministries

> She is clothed with strength and dignity;
> she can laugh at the days to come.

PROVERBS 31:25

Proverbs 31 Ministries is a nondenominational, nonprofit Christian ministry that seeks to lead women into a personal relationship with Christ. With Proverbs 31:10-31 as a guide, Proverbs 31 Ministries reaches women in the middle of their busy days through free devotions, podcast episodes, speaking events, conferences, resources, online Bible studies and training in the call to write, speak and lead others.

We are real women offering real-life solutions to those striving to maintain life's balance, in spite of today's hectic pace and cultural pull away from godly principles.

Wherever a woman may be on her spiritual journey, Proverbs 31 Ministries exists to be a trusted friend who understands the challenges she faces and walks by her side, encouraging her as she walks toward the heart of God.

Visit us online today at proverbs31.org!

Proverbs 31
MINISTRIES

LOOKING FOR YOUR NEXT STUDY?

Join us for:

How Do I Get Through This?

Pressing On When You Want To Turn Back, Give Up or Walk Away

An Exodus Study Guide

AVAILABLE MARCH 2021 AT
P31BOOKSTORE.COM